BRITANNICA LATINA

2000 YEARS OF BRITISH LATIN

Mark Walker

Tu valeas fili, valeas bene mi Gulielme,
Carior es mihi quam pocula plena theae!

First published 2009

The History Press
The Mill, Brimscombe Port
Stroud, Gloucestershire, GL5 2QG
www.thehistorypress.co.uk

© Mark Walker, 2009

The right of Mark Walker to be identified as the Author
of this work has been asserted in accordance with the
Copyrights, Designs and Patents Act 1988.

British Library Cataloguing in Publication Data.
A catalogue record for this book is available from the British Library.

ISBN 978 0 7524 5160 2

Typesetting and origination by The History Press
Printed in Malta

CONTENTS

INTRODUCTION

It's time for British Latinists to reclaim their heritage. Latin in Britain was not just the language of churchmen and lawyers; British Latin consists of more than just dusty legal documents and antiquated hymns. From Gildas and Bede to Bourne and Landor, from the earliest histories of Britain to the scientific discoveries of recent centuries, Anglo-Latin thrived as a living literary tradition. It regaled us with tales of King Arthur and the miracles of saints; it gave expression to the inductive method and the law of universal gravitation; it produced poetry and plays both serious and satirical. In short, British writers wrote pretty much anything and everything in Latin.

The focus of the modern Classics curriculum on ancient Roman writers of Latin has kept this massive and often highly enjoyable *corpus* of Anglo-Latin hidden from all but the most dedicated of academic researchers. And in the wider community the very idea that Latin flourished long after the Romans left these shores forever is generally greeted with incredulity. 'What's the point of learning Latin?' everyone asks scornfully, thinking it nothing more than the dead language of the departed conquerors. But if only they realised how much Latin has been written by British authors, they might just think again.

Britannica Latina, therefore, has two modest aims. Firstly it sets out to present what is hopefully an entertaining selection of largely unfamiliar texts, all of which (save the Roman writers of the first chapter) are from British sources. Secondly, it demonstrates by way of these selections just how vital a part Latin played in the history and literature of Britain – and therefore how vital it is to retain Latin as part of our native *British* heritage. To neglect Latin as we routinely do in British classrooms and universities is not only to neglect the classics of ancient Rome, but also to cast a dark shadow over a great deal of the cultural life of these islands.

ABOUT THIS BOOK

I have organised the selections under headings serving as more or less vaguely defined rubrics for the contents of each chapter, which proceed in rough chronological fashion from the Roman conquest to the present day. There is nothing systematic about my choice of texts –

I have chosen them for their intrinsic interest alone and not attempted to give anything like a representative selection of the many different kinds of British Latin (a task that would have been impossible in such a small book anyway). Nor have I duplicated any texts or authors featured in my previous book, *Annus Mirabilis* – hence no Vindolanda tablets or Bath curses, no William Camden or Thomas More, no John Milton or Samuel Johnson. Readers should not assume, therefore, that the authors featured here are somehow the most important of British Latinists; a different editor could quite easily have come up with an entirely different but equally rewarding selection of British Latin.

The grammatical notes are rather more spartan than in *Annus Horribilis* (which was intended for beginners) and *Annus Mirabilis*, partly for reasons of space and partly because I have assumed a fair amount of knowledge on the part of the reader – at least the ability to know how and where to look things up in a grammar book! Though English translations are provided for reference at the end of the book, and most out of the ordinary words are glossed in the notes, if you don't already possess a good dictionary (i.e. one without the words 'shorter' or 'concise' in the title) now might be a good time to consider getting one. Given the many verse selections throughout the book I did think readers would find useful a short appendix on Latin poetry.

I am very grateful to all the living Latin authors who have kindly (and *gratis*) allowed their work to be printed in the final chapter. Their dedication to the delightful art of Latin poetry is a salutary reminder that Anglo-Latin lives on today.

TIMELINE OF EVENTS, AUTHORS AND PUBLICATIONS

BC

*c.*325	Pytheas circumnavigates Britain
*c.*100–44	Gaius Julius Caesar
55 & 54	Caesar's two British expeditions

AD

43	Claudius invades Britain
49	Memorial inscription to Claudius' conquest
61–65	Julius Classicianus procurator of Britain
*c.*45–80	Cogidubnus king of the Regnenses
*c.*283/304?	Martydom of St Alban
*c.*390/461/493?	St Patrick
400–410	Roman troops withdraw from Britain
449	Angles and Saxons invade
*c.*450	Patrick's *Confessio*
*c.*504–570	St Gildas
516	Battle of Mount Badon
521–597	St Columba
*c.*540s?	Gildas' *De Excidio et Conquestu Britanniae*
*c.*624–704	Adamnan, biographer of St Columba
*c.*672–735	Bede
*c.*690	Adamnan's *Vita Sancti Columbae*
731	Bede, *Historia Ecclesiastica Gentis Anglorum*
*c.*769–?	Nennius
*c.*830	Nennius' *Historia Brittonum*
1057	Lady Godiva rides through Coventry
1066	The Battle of Hastings
*c.*1080/96–*c.*1143	William of Malmesbury
*c.*1100–*c.*1155	Geoffrey of Monmouth (*Galfridus Artur Monemutensis*)
1104	Cuthbert's relics at Durham Cathedral
1118–1170	St Thomas Becket
*c.*1120	William of Malmesbury's *Gesta Regum Anglorum*
post–1129	Simeon of Durham dies
*c.*1136	Geoffrey of Monmouth's *Historia Regum Britanniae*
*c.*1140–*c.*1208/10	Walter Map (*Gualteri Mapes*)
*c.*1146–*c.*1223	Gerald of Wales (*Giraldus Cambrensis*)
*c.*1150	Geoffrey of Monmouth's *Vita Merlini*
1157–1217	Alexander Neckam
1170	Becket assassinated at Canterbury
*c.*1180	Grim's *Vita Sanctae Thomae*; Neckam's *De naturis rerum*

1184	Joseph of Exeter
1190	'King Arthur's bones' at Glastonbury
c.1190	Joseph of Exeter's *Antiocheis*
c.1193	Map's *De Nugis Curialium* completed
c.1200–1259	Matthew Paris
c.1214–1294	Roger Bacon
1215	Signing of the *Magna Carta*
c.1223	Gerald of Wales' *De Instructione Principis*
c.1235	Roger of Wendover's *Flores Historiarum*
1236	Roger of Wendover dies
1267	Bacon's *Opus Maius*
c.1250–9	Paris' *Chronica Maiora* and *Historia Anglorum*
1506–1582	George Buchanan
1535–1607	Thomas Legge
1539/46–1600	John Case
1561–1626	Francis Bacon
1575–1621/2	George Ruggle
1578–1657	William Harvey
1579	Legge's *Ricardus Tertius*
1581–1612	Elizabeth Weston
1588	Case's *Apologia Musices*
1593–1633	George Herbert
1608	Weston's *Parthenica*
1615	Ruggle's *Ignoramus*
1620	Bacon's *Novum Organum*
1627	Herbert's *Parentalia* written
1628	Harvey's *de Motu Cordis et Sanguinis*
1643–1727	Isaac Newton
1667–1745	Jonathan Swift
1670–1726	Anthony Alsop
1687	Newton's *Principia*
1694–1747	Vincent Bourne
1698–1770	John Jortin
1734	Bourne's *Poematia*
1752	Alsop's *Odarum Libri Duo*
1775–1864	Walter Savage Landor
1847	Landor's *Poemata et Inscriptiones*
1992	Lelièvre and Huxley's *Across Bin Brook*
1995	Lelièvre's *Serus Vindemitor*
2004	Neo-Latin anthology *Alaudae*
2009	Lelièvre's *Rarae Uvae*

CHAPTER 1

THE ROMANS IN BRITAIN

In the fourth century BC a Greek explorer, Pytheas of Massilia (modern Marseilles), set off northwards on an unprecedented voyage into the unknown; he reached Cornwall and saw the natives mining tin, then astonishingly made a complete circumnavigation of the British Isles, during which he heard about distant Thule (Iceland?) from the natives of Scotland, saw Ireland from afar, and estimated the shape of the island as roughly triangular. So fantastic was his journey that when the intrepid adventurer returned to civilisation no one quite believed him and his account was ignored for centuries.

Hence when Roman traders began to follow in Pytheas' wake during the first century BC they established trading relations with the Cornish tin miners but did not venture any further. By the time Julius Caesar turned his attention to the Channel crossing, Britain still remained *terra incognita*. Even after Caesar's two expeditions (55 and 54 BC), the Romans' knowledge of Britain remained sketchy. It was not until well after the later Claudian conquest that a Roman fleet sailed round the north of Scotland and finally confirmed Pytheas' account that this new province of Britannia was indeed an island.

1. THE ROMANS FORCE A LANDING ON BRITISH SOIL (GAIUS JULIUS CAESAR, *c.* 100–44 BC)

Caesar's motives for mounting a daring raid on Britain were complicated. In the first-hand account he has left us of his ten-year campaign to conquer all of Gaul, he gives as his reason that British warriors had supported rebellious Gauls, and so Britain represented a threat to the security of his new Gallic conquests. Suetonius on the other hand claims that Caesar was tempted to make the crossing *spe margaritarum*, having heard reports of rich pearl fisheries. At least as credible is Caesar's desire for glory combined with an astute political calculation that such a deed would help keep the Senate and people on his side. Despite courting disaster during the trip, Caesar's first British expedition won him an unprecedented 20 days of thanksgiving at Rome.

This famous extract from Book 4 of *De Bello Gallico* opens as his fleet are attempting to land troops on British soil for the first time, probably somewhere near Deal in Kent. In a scene reminiscent of the D-Day landings of 1944, the Roman troops are hindered by the native tribes, who know the shores well and have gathered to oppose the invasion. As we join the story the standard-bearer of the tenth legion is encouraging his hesitant comrades to leap over the side and follow him to shore.

Atque nostris militibus cunctantibus, maxime propter altitudinem maris, qui decimae legionis aquilam ferebat, contestatus deos, ut ea res legioni feliciter eveniret, 'Desilite,' inquit, 'milites, nisi vultis aquilam hostibus prodere; ego certe meum rei publicae atque imperatori officium praestitero.' Hoc cum voce magna dixisset, se ex navi proiecit atque in hostes aquilam ferre coepit. Tum nostri cohortati inter se, ne tantum dedecus admitteretur, universi ex navi desiluerunt. Hos item ex proximis navibus cum conspexissent, subsecuti hostibus appropinquaverunt.

Pugnatum est ab utrisque acriter. Nostri tamen, quod neque ordines servare neque firmiter insistere neque signa subsequi poterant atque alius alia ex navi quibuscumque signis occurrerat se adgregabat, magnopere perturbabantur; hostes vero, notis omnibus vadis, ubi ex litore aliquos singulares ex navi egredientes conspexerant, incitatis equis impeditos adoriebantur, plures paucos circumsistebant, alii ab latere aperto in universos tela coniciebant. Quod cum animadvertisset Caesar, scaphas longarum navium, item speculatoria navigia militibus compleri iussit, et quos laborantes conspexerat, his subsidia submittebat. Nostri, simul in arido constiterunt, suis omnibus consecutis, in hostes impetum fecerunt atque eos in fugam dederunt; neque longius prosequi potuerunt, quod equites cursum tenere atque insulam capere non potuerant. Hoc unum ad pristinam fortunam Caesari defuit.

[*De Bello Gallico*, 4.25–6]

Notes:

1. cunctantibus – the soldiers hesitate to jump into the deep water
2. contestatus deos – 'having called the gods to witness'
3. praestitero – future perfect, i.e. afterwards he will be able to say that he did his duty (*meum officium*)
4. pugnatum est – impersonal passive, 'the battle was fought keenly on both sides'
5. alius alia ex navi – 'any man from any ship attached himself (*se adgregabat*) to whatever standards (*quibuscumque signis*) he had chanced upon (*occurrerat*)'
6. notis omnibus vadis – the enemy knew all the shallows

7. aliquos singulares – some Romans were jumping into the sea one by one rather than in an organised body; *incitatis equis* – the Britons spurred on their horses; *impeditos* – the troops burdened by their heavy equipment

8. Caesar – Caesar always refers to himself in the third person

9. scaphas – small boats (English 'skiffs') belonging to the warships; *speculatoria navigia* – scout ships

10. subsidia – 'he sent reinforcements to those (*his*) whom he had seen in distress (*quos laborantes conspexerat*)'

11. quod equites cursum tenere – 'because the cavalry (who were still on their ships) could not maintain their course'

12. ad pristinam fortunam Caesari defuit – 'Caesar lacked his previous good fortune'.

2. CLAUDIUS CONQUERS BRITAIN (SUETONIUS, 69–?)

After Caesar's raids Britain remained unconquered for almost a century, until the insecure Emperor Claudius decided that he needed a victory in order to win the favour of a restless Senate and fickle populace. Caligula had previously contemplated a British invasion in AD 40 but only got as far as the Channel. Claudius completed the task in 43, journeying in person to Britain, where he spent just 16 days in a bloodless conquest, before hurrying home to celebrate his triumph and adopt the honorary name *Britannicus*. Gibbon summarises the remainder of the British campaign:

> After a war of about forty years, undertaken by the most stupid, maintained by the most dissolute, and terminated by the most timid of all the emperors, the far greater part of the island submitted to the Roman yoke. The various tribes of Britons possessed valour without conduct, and the love of freedom without the spirit of union. They took up arms with savage fierceness; they laid them down, or turned them against each other with wild inconstancy; and while they fought singly, they were successively subdued. Neither the fortitude of Caractacus, nor the despair of Boadicea, nor the fanaticism of the Druids, could avert the slavery of their country.
>
> [Gibbon, *Decline and Fall*, Chapter I]

As the extract below makes clear, the waspish Roman biographer Suetonius didn't think much of Claudius' one and only expedition.

Expeditionem unam omnino suscepit eamque modicam. Cum decretis sibi a senatu ornamentis triumphalibus leviorem maiestati principali titulum arbitraretur velletque iusti triumphi decus, unde adquireret Britanniam potissimum elegit, neque temptatam ulli post Diuum Iulium et tunc tumultuantem ob non redditos transfugas. Huc cum ab Ostia navigaret, vehementi circio bis paene demersus est, prope Liguriam iuxtaque Stoechadas insulas. Quare a Massilia Gesoriacum usque pedestri itinere confecto inde transmisit ac sine ullo proelio aut sanguine intra paucissimos dies parte insulae in deditionem recepta, sexto quam profectus erat mense Romam rediit triumphavitque maximo apparatu.

[*Divus Claudius* 17.1–2]

Notes:

1. modicam – 'unimpressive', Suetonius doesn't even damn with faint praise
2. cum … arbitraretur – 'since he judged', that the triumphal regalia (*ornamentis triumphalibus*) which had been decreed to him by the Senate was an award (*titulum*) too slight (*leviorem*) for his imperial majesty (*maiestati principali*)
3. potissimum elegit – he selected (*elegit*) Britain as the place most likely (*potissimum*)
4. temptatam … transfugas – Claudius's reasons were firstly that its conquest had not been attempted (*temptatam*, agreeing with *Britanniam*) since Julius Caesar, and secondly that at the time the island was in uproar (*tumultuantem*) because a pro-Roman Briton by the name of Bericus (or Verica) and his comrades had sought Roman protection after his anti-Roman enemies Caractacus and Togodumnus had driven him from his kingdom; the Romans refused to hand back the fugitives (*non redditos transfugas*), and the tumult this caused provided an excuse for invasion
5. ab Ostia – the preposition *ab* with the place name indicates that he sailed 'from the vicinity' of the Roman port at the mouth of the Tiber
6. vehementi circio – 'a violent circular wind', the Mistral
7. prope Liguriam – his ship was almost sunk near the coast of northern Italy
8. a Massilia Gesoriacum – he therefore travelled overland (*pedestri itinere*) from Marseilles (*a Massilia*) to Boulogne (*Gesoriacum*)
9. in deditionem – in a clever literary mirroring of Claudius' hasty visit, the actual bloodless conquest (*sine ullo proelio aut sanguine*) and surrender of part of the island (*parte insulae in deditionem recepta*) is reported almost parenthetically, the main clause focusing on Claudius' return to Rome to celebrate his triumph with the greatest pomp (*maximo apparatu*)

10. sexto quam profectus erat mense – 'in the sixth month after he had set out'.

3. EARLY BRITISH INSCRIPTIONS

(a) Claudius' conquest

This text is reproduced in William Camden's *Britannia* (for which, see *Annus Mirabilis*, Chapter 6). Camden records that during the reign of Henry VIII a ploughman in Somersetshire turned up a lead sheet (*oblonga plumbi lamina*) with these words inscribed on it. Noting that Claudius also issued gold and silver coins with the same legend, *De Britannis*, Camden surmises that it was originally sited on a *tropaeum*, a commemorative trophy to Claudius' victory over the Britons.

TI. CLAVDIVS CAESAR AVG P.M.
TRIB. P.VIIII IMP. XVI. DE BRITAN.

Expanded:

Tiberius Claudius Caesar Augustus Pontifex Maximus tribunicia potestate VIIII imperator XVI de Britannis.

Notes:

1. tribunicia potestate VIIII – 'invested with the power of a tribune for the ninth time'; this sets the date at AD 49
2. imperator – 'hailed as leader for the sixteenth time'
3. de Britannis – an alternative reading is *de Britannicis fodinis*, 'from the British lead mines'.

(b) Cogidubnus inscription, Chichester

Cogidubnus (or Togidubnus) was a British client-king of the Romans whose centre of power was Fishbourne palace in West Sussex. The Roman historian Tacitus calls him *Cogidumnus* and describes him as *fidissimus*. This inscription on a marble slab was discovered in 1723 in Chichester.

[N]EPTVNO ET MINERVAE
TEMPLVM
[PR]O SALVTE DO[MVS] DIVINAE

[EX] AVCTORITA[TE TI.] CLAVD.
[CO]GIDVBNI R[EG. MA]GNI BRIT.
[COLLE]GIVM FABROR. ET [Q]VI IN E[O]
[SVN]T D. S. D. DONANTE AREAM
[?CLEM]ENTE PVDENTINI FIL.

Expanded:

Neptuno et Minervae templum pro salute domus divinae ex auctoritate Tiberii Claudii Cogidubni Regis Magni Britanniae collegium fabrorum et qui in eo sunt de suo dederunt donante aream Clemente Pudentini filii.

The words in square parentheses are conjectural reconstructions. The fifth line was formerly believed to read:

Cogidubni R(egis) Legat(i) Aug(usti) in Brit(anniae).
'of Cogidubnus King Legate of Augustus in Britain.'

Notes:

1. collegium fabrorum – 'the college of artificers and its members provided (*dederunt*) this *templum* dedicated to Neptune and Minerva'
2. donante aream – Clemens (if that is the right reading) donated the land.

(c) The tomb of Julius Classicianus, London

Julius Classicianus was appointed procurator of Britain by Nero in 61; he died in London four years later and his wife Julia Pacata erected a magnificent memorial on what is now Tower Hill, part of which was rediscovered in 1852 and a further fragment in 1935. It can now be seen in the British Museum.

DIS

MANIBUS

C IVL C F FAB ALPINI CLASSICIANI

...

...

PROC PROVINC BRITANNIAE

IVLIA INDI FILIA PACATA I ...

VXOR F

Expanded:

Dis Manibus Caii Iulii Cai Filii Fabia Tribu Alpini Classiciani ... procuratoris Provinciae Britanniae Iulia Indi filia Pacata I ... uxor fecit.

Notes:

1. Dis Manibus – the traditional invocation to the departed spirits (*Di Manes*)
2. Fabia tribu – 'in the Fabian tribe' Roman citizens were divided into 35 voting tribes
3. I ... – conjecturally *Infelix*, 'unfortunate'.

(d) A word square, Cirencester

This now famous four-times palindrome was found inscribed on a piece of wall plaster in the Roman city of Corinium (Cirencester). Other examples have been discovered in various locations across the Roman Empire, including Herculaneum and Dura-Europos in Syria. Although its exact use remains obscure, such word squares were used in the ancient world as magical charms. Speculation that this particular one is a Christian symbol has been encouraged by various imaginative rearrangements of the letters – for example spelling the phrase *Pater Noster* in a cross pattern both horizontally and vertically (with the 'n' of *noster* in the middle), either omitting the letters A and O (the Alpha and Omega) or placing them at the ends of each arm of the cross. Others argue for a Mithraic origin (the mystery cult of Mithras being a rival to the early Christian sect) or assign numerical values to the letters. One thing only is certain: lack of an obvious translation leaves the door open to innumerable interpretations.

R	O	T	A	S
O	P	E	R	A
T	E	N	E	T
A	R	E	P	O
S	A	T	O	R

Notes:

1. Arepo – to make a single, translatable sentence the word *Arepo* has to be taken as a proper name, nominative in agreement with *sator*, 'the

sower'; this is the only example ever found of the name Arepo, which
was thus probably invented solely to fit into this pattern

2.   opera – possibly ablative of *opera*, 'work, effort'.

For other examples of the very earliest British-Latin texts, see the Vindolanda
letters and curse tablets in *Annus Mirabilis*, Chapter 1, as well as more Romano-
British inscriptions in *Annus Horribilis*, Chapter 14.

4. THE ROMANS LEAVE FOREVER (GILDAS, *c.*504–570)

At the beginning of the fifth century, pressure from the Goths on the
Roman frontiers caused the Emperor Honorius (395–423) gradually
to withdraw troops from Britain, until by 410 – the year in which the
Goths sacked Rome itself – the island province was finally abandoned
and left to organise its own defence against the ravages of the Picts,
Scots and Saxons.

'A monk, who, in the profound ignorance of human life, has presumed
to exercise the office of historian, strangely disfigures the state of Britain
at the time of its separation from the Western empire. Gildas describes
in florid language … the sinful luxury of the British people; of a people,
according to the same writer, ignorant of the most simple arts, and
incapable, without the aid of the Romans, of providing walls of stone,
or weapons of iron, for the defence of their native land.' Gibbon, *Decline
and Fall*, Chapter XXXVIII

Gildas (St Gildas the Wise), despite being closer to the events he relates than
any other source, has a rather shaky grasp of both facts and chronology:
he wrongly places the withdrawal of Roman troops during the reign of
the usurper Maximus (383–388), and describes how the Roman army
encouraged the British to build defensive walls – actually the far older
Antonine and Hadrianic walls – at this time. Gildas is indeed less a historian
than a Christian moralist, and his *De Excidio et Conquestu Britanniae*, 'On
the ruin and conquest of Britain', is more a sermon than an historical
account, according to which the depredations of the invaders are God's
punishment for the luxury and licentiousness of the decadent British.

Here he is relating the story of three appeals to Rome by the recently abandoned British, two of which were answered when Roman legions returned to repel invading Scots and Picts. As we take up the tale, the Romans have for a second time driven the hostile tribes out of the province, but worn out by the effort, they now decide it is high time that the British started defending themselves.

Igitur Romani, patriae denuntiantes nequaquam se tam laboriosis expeditionibus posse frequentius vexari, et ob imbelles erraticosque latrunculos, Romana stigmata, tantum talemque exercitum terra ac mari fatigari; sed ut potius sola consuescendo armis ac viriliter dimicando terram substantiolam coniuges liberos et, quod his maius est, libertatem vitamque totis viribus vindicaret et gentibus nequaquam sibi fortioribus, nisi segnitia et torpore dissolveretur, inermes vinculis vinciendas nullo modo, sed instructas peltis ensibus hastis et ad caedam promptas protenderet manus, suadentes, quia et hoc putabant aliquid derelinquendo populo commodi adcrescere, murum non ut alterum, sumptu publico privatoque adiunctis secum miserabilibus indigenis, solito structurae more, tramite a mari usque ad mare inter urbes, quae ibidem forte ob metum hostium collocatae fuerant, directo librant; fortia formidoloso populo monita tradunt, exemplaria instituendorum armorum relinquunt. In litore quoque oceani ad meridianam plagam, quo naves eorum habebantur, quia et inde barbaricae ferae bestiae timebantur, turres per intervalla ad prospectum maris collocant, et valedicunt tamquam ultra non reversuri.

[*De Excidio et Conquestu Britanniae,* 18]

Notes:

1. patriae denuntiantes – the Romans announce their intention to Britain (*patriae*); *nequaquam* – 'by no means'; Bede in his *Historia Ecclesiastica* writes: '*tum Romani denuntiavere Brettonibus non se ultra ob eorum defensionem tam laboriosis expeditionibus posse fatigari*'

2. frequentius – 'any longer'

3. Romana stigmata – the Romans have already set their brand upon these 'unwarlike and wandering bandits (*imbelles erraticosque latrunculos*)', i.e. they have defeated them

4. ut … vindicaret – purpose clause; *sola* – i.e. Britain on its own should lay claim (*vindicaret*) to its subsistence land (*terram substantiolem*) etc.

5. consuescendo … dimicando – 'by becoming accustomed … by fighting'

6. quod his maius est – 'what is greater than these'

7. dissolveretur – continuation of the purpose clause introduced by *ut*: 'that they not be divided by stronger nations (*gentibus fortioribus*)'

8. protenderet – also clause of purpose; Gildas' syntax is rather convoluted and requires careful unpicking: 'Britain should stretch forth its hands', which are not 'unarmed to be bound (*inermes vinciendas*)' but rather 'equipped with shields etc. (*instructas peltis …*)' and 'readily inclined to slaughter (*ad caedem promptas*)'

9. suadentes – so the Romans recommend

10. aliquid … commodi – 'something of benefit to the people being deserted (*derelinquendo populo*)'

11. murum – accusative after greatly delayed verb *librant*, literally 'make level', a surveyor's term, i.e. 'they build a level wall unlike the other one (*non ut alterum*)' – they have already helped the natives build a less solid wall, but this one is made of brick (*solito structurae more*); *tramite … directo* – 'with its course having been arranged/fixed'; *a mari usque ad mare* – he means Hadrian's wall

12. fortia … monita – they give words of courage to the frightened people

13. ad meridianam plagam – south-facing; *barbaricae ferae bestiae* – the Saxon invaders come from that direction

14. exemplaria – patterns for fabricating arms; the Britons don't even know how to make their own weapons

15. tamquam – parenthetical, 'so to speak', since the Romans probably didn't actually say 'Goodbye!'.

RECOMMENDED READING

Caesar (ed. John)   ***Caesar's Expedition to Britain 55 & 54 BC***
Bristol Classical Press

Book 4 of *De Bello Gallico*, with notes and commentary by D.A.S. John.

Gildas (ed. Williams)   ***De Excidio Britanniae etc.***

Facsimile reprint of an 1899 edition.

CHAPTER 2

BRITISH HISTORY

After the collapse of the Roman province, Roman government, Roman law, Roman education and all the other benefits of Roman occupation (no need to ask what the Romans had done for Britain), the former province began to decline rapidly. By the middle of the fifth century most of the urban centres had fallen into decay and disuse, the populace scattered or destroyed either by the Anglo-Saxon invaders or the plague or both. Even the use of money was replaced by a system of barter. The church retained a tenuous grip on some centres in the remote Celtic parts of the Scottish highlands and islands, thanks to the ministry of St Columba (Chapter 4), and it was the church which kept the guttering flame of learning alight, though dimly, in their monasteries. Not surprising, then, that the early historians of Britain were monks to a man.

1. THE ARRIVAL OF THE ANGLO-SAXONS (BEDE, c.672–735)

The greatest of the medieval historians, Bede, spent most of his life at the monastery of St Paul in Jarrow where he wrote principally on theological matters. But his *Historia Ecclesiastica*, although ostensibly an account of the establishment of Christianity in Britain, ranges far wider across British history. He derives his posthumous epithet 'Venerable' from a legend that relates how a monk tried to carve a hexameter epitaph on his tomb and managed to produce '*Hac sunt in fossa Baedae … ossa*', but was stuck for a word to fill the last syllable of the fourth and the fifth foot (see Appendix for hexameters). He gave up the attempt and went to bed, only to find that in the morning an angel (not another monk, no) had visited the tomb and inserted the word '*venerabilis*'.

'The British writers assign one cause which facilitated the entrance of the Saxons into this island; the love with which Vortigern was at first seized for Rovena, the daughter of Hengist, and which that artful warrior

> made use of to blind the eyes of the imprudent monarch. The same
> historians add ... that Vortigern accepted of a banquet from Hengist, at
> Stonehenge, where 300 of his nobility were treacherously slaughtered,
> and himself detained captive.' David Hume, *History of England*

In this extract from Bede's history, as in many other places, he follows
Gildas' narrative quite closely but tells the story with somewhat more
elegance. The British King Vortigern, in an attempt to deal with the
continual incursions of the northern tribes, has made a disastrous decision
– he has invited the Germanic tribes of Angles and Saxons to come to
Britain and help fight against the Scots and Picts; this they willingly
do, led by their generals Hengist and Horsa. But no sooner have they
arrived than they turn their weapons against the British. The year is 449:

*Tum subito inito ad tempus foedere cum Pictis, quos longius iam bellando pepulerant,
in socios arma vertere incipiunt; et primum quidem annonas sibi eos affluentius
ministrare cogunt, quaerentesque occasionem divortii, protestantur, nisi profusior sibi
alimentorum copia daretur, se cuncta insulae loca, rupto foedere, vastaturos; neque
aliquanto segnius minas effectibus prosequuntur. Siquidem, ut breviter dicam, accensus
manibus paganorum ignis, iustas de sceleribus populi Dei ultiones expetiit, non illius
impar qui quondam a Chaldaeis succensus Hierosolymorum moenia, immo aedificia
cuncta consumsit. Sic enim et hic agente impio victore, immo disponente iusto Iudice,
proximas quasque civitates agrosque depopulans, ab orientali mari usque ad occidentale,
nullo prohibente, suum continuavit incendium, totamque prope insulae pereuntis
superficiem obtexit. Ruebant aedificia publica simul et privata, passim sacerdotes inter
altaria trucidabantur, praesules cum populis sine ullo respectu honoris, ferro pariter et
flammis absumebantur; nec erat, qui crudeliter interemptos sepulturae traderet. Itaque
nonnulli de miserandis reliquiis in montibus comprehensi, acervatim iugulabantur; alii
fame confecti procedentes manus hostibus dabant, pro accipiendis alimentorum subsidiis
aeternum subituri servitium, si tamen non continuo trucidarentur; alii transmarinas
regiones dolentes petebant; alii perstantes in patria trepidi pauperem vitam in montibus,
silvis, vel rupibus arduis, suspecta semper mente agebant.*

*At ubi hostilis exercitus, exterminatis dispersisque insulae indigenis, domum
reversus est, coeperunt et illi paulatim vires animosque resumere, emergentes de
latibulis, quibus abditi fuerant, et unanimo consensu auxilium coeleste precantes,
ne usque ad internecionem usquequaque delerentur. Utebantur eo tempore duce
Ambrosio Aureliano, viro modesto, qui solus forte Romanae gentis praefatae tempestati*

superfuerat, occisis in eadem parentibus regium nomen et insigne ferentibus. Hoc ergo
duce, vires capessunt Brittones, et victores provocantes ad proelium victoriam ipsi,
Deo favente, suscipiunt; et ex eo tempore nunc cives, nunc hostes vincebant, usque
ad annum obsessionis Badonici montis, quando non minimas eisdem hostibus strages
dabant, quadragesimo circiter et quarto anno adventus eorum in Brittaniam.

[*Historia Ecclesiastica Gentis Anglorum*, 1.15–16]

Notes:

1. inito ... foedere – 'having entered into a treaty'; *ad tempus* – 'for the time being'

2. affluentius – 'in greater abundance'

3. occasionem divortii – 'seeking an opportunity for a quarrel'

4. protestantur – deponent, 'they publicly declared that ...', followed by accusative + infinitive *se vastaturos* (sc. *esse*)

5. neque aliquanto segnius – 'by no means tardily did they follow (*prosequuntur*) their threats (*minas*) with actions (*effectibus*)'

6. expetiit – 'which exacted the righteous retribution (*iustas ultiones*) of God'

7. Chaldaeis – 'And the Chaldeans burned the king's house, and the houses of the people, with fire, and brake down the walls of Jerusalem' (*Jeremiah*, 39:8); like the inhabitants of Jerusalem, Bede argues, the British deserved God's punishment for their sins

8. agente impio victore – 'with the impious conqueror (i.e. the Saxons) behaving in the same way (*sic*, i.e. as the Chaldeans) here as well (*et hic*)'

9. praesules – bishops (*praesul* in Classical Latin = a dancer who leads a religious procession)

10. qui ... sepulturae traderet – 'anyone who could deliver for burial those cruelly murdered (*crudeliter interemptos*)'

11. miserandis reliquiis – 'the pitiful remnants'; *acervatim* – 'in heaps'

12. manus ... dabant – surrendered themselves (*manus dare* = 'to surrender'); *subituri* – future participle of *subeo*; in return for food they were to endure eternal slavery

13. suspecta mente – 'feeling apprehensive'; *suspectus* = 'suspicious, mistrustful'

14. quibus abditi fuerant – 'where they had hidden themselves'

15. usque ad internecionem – 'to the point of extermination'

16. utebantur – 'they took as their leader'; *utor* + ablative

17. Ambrosio Aureliano – Aurelius Ambrosius, first mentioned by Gildas, whose account Bede is following here; a Romano-British leader who

in Geoffrey of Monmouth's history (Chapter 3) is identified as King Arthur's uncle

18. superfuerat – takes dative *praefatae tempestati*, 'he alone had survived the aforementioned storm', though his parents were killed

19. Badonici montis – Mount Badon, the victory ascribed by Ennius (Chapter 3) to King Arthur in AD 516.

2. THE TYRANNICAL RULERS OF BRITAIN (GILDAS, *c.* 504–570)

Returning to Gildas, whose account of the departure of the Romans is given in Chapter 1, we are presented with an unremittingly gloomy portrait of Britain in the author's own day. No sign here of the glories of King Arthur's Camelot, just tyrants and impious barons who oppress the poor. One is irresistibly reminded of the peasant's cry in the film *Monty Python and the Holy Grail*, 'Come and see the violence inherent in the system! Help, help, I'm being repressed!'

Reges habet Britannia, sed tyrannos; iudices habet, sed impios; saepe praedantes et concutientes, sed innocentes; vindicantes et patrociniantes, sed reos et latrones; quamplurimas coniuges habentes, sed scortantes et adulterantes; crebro iurantes, sed periurantes; voventes, et continue propemodum mentientes; belligerantes, sed civila et iniusta bella agentes; per patriam quidem fures magnopere insectantes, et eos, qui secum ad mensam sedent, latrones, non solum amantes, sed et munerantes; eleemosynas largiter dantes, sed e regione immensum montem scelerum exaggerantes; in sede arbitraturi sedentes, sed raro recti iudicii regulam quaerentes; innoxios humilesque despicientes; sanguinarios superbos, parricidas commanipulares et adulteros Dei inimicos, si sors, ut dicitur, tulerit, qui cum ipso nomine certatim delendi erant, ad sidera, prout possunt, efferentes; vinctos plures in carceribus habentes, quos dolo sui potius quam merito proterunt catenis onerantes; inter altaria iurando demorantes, et haec eadem ac si lutulenta paulo post saxa despicientes.

[*De Excidio Et Conquestu Britanniae: Epistola Gildae*, 27]

Notes:

1. note the frequent, almost poetical, use of the present participle referring to the *reges* and *iudices*

2. innocentes – 'free from blame'; the first of a series of antithetical statements: they are plunderers and intimidators (*praedantes et concutientes*)

yet they remain blameless, since there is no one (except Gildas) to judge them

3. vindicantes et patrociniantes – though they themselves are guilty robbers (*reos at latrones*) they act as defenders and advocates

4. scortantes – 'consorting with prostitutes'

5. crebro iurantes – though perjurers (*periurantes*) they repeatedly take oaths

6. voventes ... mentientes – 'making vows ... telling lies'

7. belligerantes – 'war-mongers', but of unjust and civil war

8. quidem fures ... latrones – 'some (*quidem*) earnestly (*magnopere*) pursue (*insectantes*) thieves, yet they (*et eos*) who sit at their tables are bandits (*latrones*) who are loved and rewarded too (*amantes, sed et munerantes*)'

9. eleemosynas – 'alms'

10. e regione – 'on the other hand'

11. exaggerantes – 'heap up'

12. arbitraturi – future participle to express purpose: 'in order to pass judgement'

13. regulam – the rule or standard of an impartial trial

14. sanguinarios ... adulteros – all accusatives of the people whom the kings and judges 'praise to the skies' (*ad sidera ... efferentes*); *commanipulares* – their fellow murderers and adulterers

15. si sors ... tulerit – 'if fate will endure it'; *ut dicitur* – 'so it is said'

16. delendi erant – gerundive of obligation: 'those who in his very name (i.e. the Lord's) certainly ought to be destroyed'

17. vinctos plures ... proterunt catenis onerantes – 'they (the kings and judges) crush (*proterunt*) their many vanquished foes (*vinctos plures*), weighing them down (*onerantes*) with chains (*catenis*)'

18. demorantes – 'they detain (*demorantes*) their enemies by swearing an oath (*iurando*) on the altars which later they despise (*despicientes*) as if they were mud-covered stones (*lutulenta ... saxa*)'.

3. LADY GODIVA (ROGER OF WENDOVER, D. 1236)

Roger of Wendover passed much of his life at St Albans Abbey. His *Flores Historiarum* is, as the title suggests, a compilation of earlier historical and ecclesiastical writings, but it does also include rather livelier material about more recent events, including the Crusades, up to 1235, the year before his death. The *Flores* continued to be added to by other chroniclers and in its final form takes events to the year 1326. In this extract, Roger relates the story of Lady Godiva, whose famous naked journey through the streets of Coventry took place in 1057.

> *Godiva vero comitissa et amatrix Dei genitricis villam Conventrensem a gravi thelonei servitute liberare affectans comitem virum suum saepe magnis precibus rogavit, ut Iesu Christi et eius genitricis intuitu villam a praedicta absolveret servitute et aliis exactionibus importunis; cumque comes increparet illam, quod rem sibi damnosam inaniter postularet, prohibuit constanter, ne ipsum super hanc rem amplius conveniret; illa e contrario pertinacia muliebri ducta virum indesinenter exasperans de praemissis tale responsum ab illo recepit, 'Ascende,' inquit, 'equum tuum nuda et transi per mercatum villae ab initio usque ad finem, populo congregato, et cum redieris, quod postulas impetrabis.' Cui Godiva respondens ait, 'Et, si hoc voluero, licentiam mihi dabis?' Ad quam ille, 'Dabo,' inquit. Tunc comitissa Deo dilecta duobus comitata militibus nuda, ut praedictum est, equum ascendens crines capitis et tricas dissolvit corpusque suum totum inde velavit, et forum pertransiens a nemine visa, apparentibus cruribus tamen candidissmis, iter complevit, et ad virum gaudens reversa, hoc factum admirantem, quod petierat impetravit; comes vero Leofricus villam Conventrensem et homines a praefata liberans servitute, per cartam suam quod fecerat confirmavit.*

> [*Chronica Sive Flores Historiarum*]

Notes:

1. comittissa – 'countess'
2. genitricis – 'the mother of God'
3. villam Conventrensem – Coventry
4. thelonei – genitive of *theloneum*, 'a toll', the right of the landlord to tax those who live on his land
5. affectans – 'endeavouring'
6. comitem virum suum – her husband, Count Leofric
7. intuitu – 'in consideration of' followed by genitives *Christi et eius genitricis*
8. increparet – 'reproached her'
9. quod ... postularet – 'that she was demanding'; *inaniter* – 'without good reason'
10. amplius conveniret – 'forbade her to approach him any more'
11. pertinacia muliebri ducta – 'led by a womanly stubbornness'
12. de praemissis – 'about the aforementioned matters'
13. ascende ... transi – imperatives

14. populo congregato – ablative absolute, 'with the people gathered round', i.e. when the marketplace was full

15. cum redieris … impetrabis – future perfect *redieris* in the *cum*-clause, as the main verb is future; English prefers present tense, 'when you return, you will obtain what you demand'

16. voluero – another future perfect where English prefers the present, 'if I am willing'

17. crines capitis et tricas dissolvit – the curls of her hair (*tricae*, 'tangles, difficulties'), which she lets down (*dissolvit*) to cover her nudity; only her lovely white legs are visible (*apparentibus cruribus candidissimis*)

18. hoc factum admirantem – her husband marvels at this deed

19. quod petierat impetravit – 'that which she had sought, she obtained'

20. per cartam – he confirmed what he had done in writing.

4. THE BATTLE OF HASTINGS (WILLIAM OF MALMESBURY, *c.* 1080/96–*c.* 1143)

Though following Bede's account closely in its earlier sections, William of Malmesbury's *Gesta Regum Anglorum* is most valued for its description of more modern times. As librarian of Malmesbury Abbey in Wiltshire, William had access to a great fund of material and used it wisely – after Bede he is the most accurate and useful of the monkish chroniclers.

In this extract, William gives us a vivid picture of the events of 14 October 1066. As we join the narrative, King Harold's English and King William's Normans are preparing for battle.

Itaque utrinque animosi duces disponunt acies, patrio quisque ritu: Angli, ut accepimus, totam noctem insomnem cantibus potibusque ducentes, mane incunctanter in hostem procedunt: pedites omnes cum bipennibus, conserta ante se scutorum testudine, impenetrabilem cuneum facient; quod profecto illis ea die saluti fuisset, nisi Normanni simulata fuga more suo confertos manipulos laxassent. Rex ipse pedes iuxta vexillum stabat cum fratribus, ut, in commune periculo aequato, nemo de fuga cogitaret. Vexillum illud post victoriam papae misit Willelmus, quod erat in hominis pugnantis figura, aure et lapidibus arte sumptuosa intextum.

Contra Normanni, nocte tota confessioni peccatorum vacantes, mane Dominico corpore communicarunt. Pedites cum arcubus et sagittis primam frontem muniunt, equites retro divisis alis consistunt. Comes vultu serenus, et clara voce suae parti utpote iustiori Deum affuturum pronuncians, arma poposcit; moxque ministrorum tumultu loricam inversam indutus, casum risu correxit, 'Vertetur,' inquiens, 'fortitudo comitatus mei in regnum.' Tunc cantilena Rollandi inchoata, ut martium viri exemplum pugnaturos accenderet, inclamatoque Dei auxilio, praelium consertum, bellatumque acriter, neutris in multam diei horam cedentibus. Quo comperto, Willelmus innuit suis, ut, ficta fuga, campo se subtraherent. Hoc commento Anglorum cuneus solutus, quasi palantes hostes a tergo caesurus, exitium sibi maturavit; Normanni enim, conversis ordinibus reversi, dispersos adoriuntur, et in fugam cogunt. Ita ingenio circumventi, pulchram mortem pro patriae ultione meruere: nec tamen ultioni suae defuere, quin, crebro consistentes, de insequentibus insignes cladis acervos facerent; nam, occupato tumulo, Normannos, calore succensos acriter ad superiora nitentes, in vallem deiiciunt, levique negotio in subiectos tela torquentes, lapides rotantes, omnes ad unum fundunt. Item fossatum quoddam praeruptum compendiario et noto sibi transitu evadentes, tot ibi inimicorum conculcavere, ut cumulo cadaverum planitiem campi aequarent. Valuit haec vicissitudo, modo illis, modo istis vincentibus, quantum Haroldi vita moram fecit; at ubi iactu sagittae violato cerebro procubuit, fuga Anglorum perennis in nocte fuit. Emicuit ibi virtus amborum ducum.

[*Gesta Regum Anglorum*, 3.241–2]

Notes:

1. disponunt – the use of the 'historic' present tense to make the action seem more vivid dates back to Caesar's accounts of his Gallic Wars (Chapter 1); *ut accepimus* – 'as we have been told'

2. ducentes – another historic present: 'having spent the entire sleepless night in singing and drinking'; *incunctanter* – 'without hesitation'

3. bipennibus – double-bladed axes

4. facient – future tense, the narrative pictures them as they advance but before they encounter the enemy

5. saluti fuisset – predicative dative with the perfect subjunctive: 'would have been a source of salvation for them (*illis*)', i.e 'would have saved them'

6. more suo – refers to the *confertos manipulos*, 'the densely packed companies'

7. contra – 'on the opposite side'

8. vacantes – contrast with the boozy English *ducentes* above; *confessioni*, dative: 'giving the whole night to the confession of their sins'

9. Dominico corpore – ablative after *communicarunt*, 'they partook of the Lord's body', i.e. they celebrated Mass

10. Deum affuturum – future accusative + infinitive (sc. *esse*), 'that God will be with them'

11. comitatus mei – genitive; *comitatus* is here synonymous with the medieval term *ducatus*, 'his dukedom', which William jokes will be turned round into a kingdom like his armour

12. cantilena Rollandi – the Song of Roland was a chivalric ballad set in the age of Charlemagne

13. pugnaturos – 'those who were about to fight'

14. in multam diei horam – 'until late in the day' or 'during the greater part of the day'

15. caesurus – agrees with *cuneus*, future participle to express purpose: 'in order to cut down the fleeing enemy'

16. conversis ordinibus – 'with their ranks faced about'; the Normans suddenly turn and attack the dispersed English

17. meruere … defuere – contracted forms of *meruerunt, defuerunt*

18. quin … facerent – 'but that they made …'

19. calore succensos – 'inflamed by zeal'

20. levique negotio – 'with little trouble'

21. ad unum – 'to a man', 'without exception'

22. fossatum … praeruptum – 'a steep ditch' which they avoided 'by a short (*compendario*) and familiar (*noto*) route'

23. conculcavere – contracted form of *conculcaverunt*, 'they trampled underfoot'

24. valuit – 'this toing and froing (*vicissitudo*) carried on for as long as Harold's life caused a delay', i.e. while Harold was alive.

5. THE SIGNING OF THE MAGNA CARTA (MATTHEW PARIS, *c.*1200–1259)

Like Roger of Wendover, Matthew Paris (*Matthaeus Parisiensis*) was a monk of St Albans Abbey, but he was also an artist whose manuscripts are prized for their remarkable watercolour illuminations. Matthew undertook a continuation of his predecessor Roger's history, bringing the story of Britain to his own day.

In this section of his *Historia Anglorum* (a distillation of his larger work, the *Chronica Maiora*), Paris follows Roger of Wendover's original account, painting an unsympathetic portrait of King John, who in 1215 was reluctantly compelled to sign an agreement with his rebellious barons; they had so denuded him of support that he was left with no choice but to submit to their terms – even though he had no intention of honouring the stipulations presented to him in the Great Charta at Runnymede.

'The two races [Normans and English], so long hostile, soon found that they had common interests and common enemies. Both were alike aggrieved by the tyranny of a bad king ... The greatgrandsons of those who had fought under William and the greatgrandsons of those who had fought under Harold began to draw near to each other in friendship; and the first pledge of their reconciliation was the Great Charter, won by their united exertions, and framed for their common benefit.' Macaulay, *History of England*.

Concessae sunt libertates in dolo, et pax facta, sed odibilis.

Rex autem se cernens iam ab fere omnibus derelictum, sibi coepit formidare vehementer, et, concepto contra ipsos odio inexorabili, simulavit in dolo se velle pacem ad tempus facere, ut cum postea fortior surrexisset, in dissipata agmina acrius se vindicaret, et qui in omnes non poterat, in singulos cautius desaeviret. Mittens igitur ad ipsos Willelmum Marescallum, comitem de Penbroc, cum aliis quibusdam fide dignis, mandavit eis benigne, quod pro bono pacis et regni sui exaltatione et promissi sui fideli complemento, concederet eis libertates, quas petebant. Ipsi vero gavisi, et falso gaudio recreati, statuerunt diem, ut veniret contra eos ad colloquium, in prato inter Stanes et Windleshores, xv. die Iunii. Quo cum pervenissent, rex benigne baronibus postulata concessit, et carta conscripsit ...

Postquam autem rex Johannes baronibus omnes libertates et leges postulatas, corde aliud parturiente, sponte quasi ex abundanti superaddidit:

'Cum autem pro Deo, et emendatione regni nostri, et ad melius sopiendam discordiam inter nos et barones nostros ortam, haec omnia concesserimus, volentes ea integra et firma stabilire, facimus et concedimus eis securitatem subscriptam, videlicet quod barones eligant xxv barones de regno, quos voluerint, qui debeant pro totis viribus suis observare, tenere, et facere observari pacem et libertates, quas eis concessimus, et hac praesenti carta nostra confirmavimus, ita scilicet quod, si nos, vel iusticiarii nostri erga aliquem in aliquo deliquerimus, vel aliquem articulorum transgressi fuerimus, et delictum fuerit ostensum quatuor baronibus de xxv, illi quatuor accedant ad nos vel ad iusticiarium nostrum, si fuerimus extra regnum,

proponentes nobis excessum, petent ut sine dilatione faciamus emendari. Quod si nos excessum non emendaverimus infra tempus xl. dierum, computando a tempore quo monstratum fuerit, praedicti quatuor barones referent causam illam ad residuos de illis xxv baronibus, et illi cum communa totius terrae distringent et gravabunt nos modis omnibus quibus potuerunt, donec fuerit emendatum secundum arbitrium eorum; salva persona nostra, et reginae et liberorum nostrorum. Et cum fuerit emendatum, intendent nobis, ut prius fecerunt.'

[*Historia Anglorum sive historia minor, De Tempore Regis Iohannis*]

Notes:

1. fortior surrexisset – John signs the Charta knowing that after he has restored his fortunes he will be able to have his revenge against the then-dispersed forces (*in dissipata agmina*) of the rebellious barons, attacking them one by one (*in singulos*)

2. Willelmum Marescallum – William Mareschal, Earl of Pembroke

3. in prato – the field of Runnymede

4. corde aliud parturiente – 'while brooding over something in his heart'; *sponte* – 'by his own volition', i.e. he adds a clause not required by the barons; *quasi ex abundanti* – 'almost as if superfluously', he wishes to disguise his real intent

5. Cum autem pro Deo – here Paris quotes verbatim clause 61 of the Charta, which established a committee of 25 barons to oversee John's reign and call him to account. John renounced its provisions almost immediately

6. ad … sopiendam – 'for the sake of calming discord'

7. quos voluerint – the future perfect tense is used throughout for things that 'will have been done'; English often prefers a simple present tense

8. pro totis viribus – 'with all their might'

9. iusticiarii – the king's chief minister, his *justiciar*, who acts as regent if the king is out of the country

10. ostensum quatuor baronibus – John's breach of contract needs only to be brought to the attention of four of the 25 barons

11. proponentes nobis excessum – 'laying before us the deviation'

12. cum communa – 'with the communal resources of the whole land'

13. modis omnibus quibus potuerunt – 'in every way they can'; *salva persona nostra* – except they are prohibited from harming the king and his family.

RECOMMENDED READING:

Bede (ed. Garforth)   *Historia Ecclesiastica* (selections)
                                    Bolchazy-Carducci

Reprint of F.W. Garforth's 1967 student edition.

Matthew Paris (ed. Giles)   *English History*
                                    Kessinger Publishing

Roger of Wendover   *Flowers of History*
(ed. Giles)   Llanerch Press

William of Malmesbury   *Chronicle of the Kings of England*
(ed. Giles)   Kessinger/BiblioBazaar

Facsimile reprints of mid-nineteenth century editions edited by
J.A. Giles.

CHAPTER 3

ARTHUR AND MERLIN

In those dark ages after the Roman withdrawal, when learning had been driven out of mainland Britain, tales were told of heroes who resisted the invading Saxons. Whether King Arthur was a real British war leader, or a fiction of the Welsh bardic singers embellished by later writers, remains a matter for debate. Countless books, not to mention movies and television documentaries, continue to embroider the basic story: that in the face of the depredations of foreign invaders during the fifth and sixth centuries, the native Britons fought back under an inspirational general. But Gildas (who should have been a contemporary of Arthur's) never mentions him; our first Latin reference to him does not occur until the early ninth century in the writings of Nennius. And what we now think of as the basis of Arthurian legend does not occur until the twelfth century and Geoffrey of Monmouth's *Historia* – all subsequent retellings and variations are indebted to his seminal account.

'Concerning all the other provinces of the Western Empire we have continuous information. It is only in Britain that an age of fable completely separates two ages of truth. Odacer and Totila, Euric and Thrasimund, Clovis, Fredegunda, and Brunechild are historical men and women. But Hengist and Horsa, Vortigern and Rowena, Arthur and Mordred are mythical persons, whose very existence may be questioned, and whose adventures must be classed with those of Hercules and Romulus.' Macaulay, *History of England*.

The Welsh also sang of a prophet and 'wild man of the woods' called 'Myrddin'. Geoffrey of Monmouth Latinised the name as 'Merlinus' (Merddin sounded too much like the French *merde*) and introduced him into his history both as a prophet (in the influential 'Prophecies of Merlin') and as a magical associate of Arthur.

1. MERLIN HELPS UTHERPENDRAGON (GEOFFREY OF MONMOUTH, *c.*1100–*c.*1155)

Geoffrey of Monmouth (*Galfridus Artur Monemutensis*) was a bishop with a real literary flair. He wrote attractive Latin in both prose and verse and his *Historia Regum Britanniae* is the most widely read of all the medieval histories, a fact that can be explained by Geoffrey's ability not only to tell a good story but also – in the absence of original sources – to make them up as well. Geoffrey claims to be translating his history from an ancient book written in the British (i.e. Welsh) language, *quendam Britannici sermonis librum vetustissimum*, though no such book can be identified. Possibly Geoffrey drew on oral and folkloric traditions to produce a work that, though mostly fiction, has some tenuous basis in historical fact; and though it might not qualify as true history, it deserves its longevity as a work of literature.

In this passage, Geoffrey's racy narrative tells of the conception of Arthur. King Utherpendragon has become enamoured of Igraine, wife of the Duke of Cornwall. Uther promptly lays siege to Cornwall, who has secured his wife in the castle of Tintagel. But Uther's lust will brook no obstacle, and he calls on Merlin for magical assistance. The incident is gloriously reenacted in John Boorman's 1981 movie *Excalibur.*

> *Vocatus confestim Merlinus, cum in praesentia regis astitisset, iussus est consilium dare, quo rex desiderium in Igerna expleret. Qui comperta anxietate quam rex patiebatur pro ea commotus est super tanto amore ipsius et ait, 'Ut voto tuo potiaris, utendum est tibi novis artibus et tempore tuo inauditis. Scio medicaminibus meis dare figuram Gorlois, ita ut per omnia ipse videaris. Si itaque parueris, faciam te prorsus simulare eum; Ulfin vero Jordanum de Tintagol familiarem eius. Alia autem specie sumpta, adero tertius, poterisque tuto oppidum adire ad Igernam, ac aditum habere.' Paruit itaque rex, diligentemque animum adhibuit. Postremo commissa familiaribus suis obsidione, se Merlini medicationibus commisit, et in speciem Gorlois transmutatus est. Mutatus est et Ulfin in Jordanum, Merlinus in Bricclem: ita ut nemini quod fuerant comparerent: deinde aggressi sunt viam versus Tintagol, et cum crepusculo ad oppidum venerunt. Indicato ocius ianitori quod consul adveniret, apertae sunt ianuae, et intromissi sunt viri. Quis enim alius accessisset, cum ipse Gorlois reputaretur adesse? Mansit itaque rex ea nocte cum Igerna, et sese desiderata Venere refecit. Deceperat namque illam falsa specie quam assumpserat; deceperat etiam ficticiis sermonibus, quos ornate componebat. Dicebat enim se egressum esse*

ab obsesso oppido, ut sibi tam dilectae rei atque oppido disponeret: unde ipsa credula nihil quod poscebatur abnegavit. Concepit itaque eadem nocte celeberrimum illum Arturum, qui postmodum ut celebris esset, mira probitate promeruit.

[*Historia Regum Britanniae*, 8.19]

Notes:

1. Igerna – Igraine, wife of Gorlois Duke of Cornwall
2. comperta anxietate – ablative absolute, 'having learnt of the anxiety …'
3. pro ea – 'because of her [Igraine]'
4. super – 'with regard to' + ablative
5. ut … potiaris – clause of purpose, 'in order to obtain your wish'; *voto tuo* is ablative after verb *potior*
6. utendum est – impersonal passive of an intransitive verb: 'You must use new methods (*novis artibus*)'
7. medicaminibus – drugs, potions
8. ut … videaris – clause of result, signposted by *ita*, 'so that you will seem'
9. per omnia – 'in every respect'
10. parueris – future perfect of *pareo*
11. oppidum – take with *ad Igernam*, 'You will be able to approach the citadel and Igraine'
12. diligentemque animum adhibuit – 'gave [Merlin] his attention diligently'
13. commissa … obsidione – ablative absolute, 'with the seige having been entrusted to'
14. Bricelem – Britaelis, another of Gorlois' companions
15. ut … comparerent – another result clause signposted by *ita*, 'so that what they had been was obvious to no one'
16. indicato … ianitori – ablative absolute, 'when it was announced to the gatekeeper'; *ocius* – comparative adverb, 'sooner than expected'
17. accessisset – pluperfect subjunctive in an indirect question
18. sese desiderata … refecit – 'achieved what he had desired for himself'; *Venere* – 'by love-making'
19. ornate – he made up high-flown speeches
20. ut … disponeret – purpose clause, 'to arrange matters for his beloved (*dilectae*) and for the town'
21. ut celebris esset … promeruit – 'deserved by his remarkable virtue to be celebrated'.

2. ARTHUR'S BATTLES (NENNIUS, *c*.769–?)

Nennius is a shadowy figure whose *Historia Brittonum* is a compilation of various earlier writings from the dark ages of British history. He is a primary source for King Arthur, preserving in abbreviated form the traditions of earlier Welsh sources. In this section, Nennius provides a summary of Arthur's battles:

> *In illo tempore Saxones invalescebant in multitudine et crescebant in Brittannia. Mortuo autem Hengisto Octha filius eius transivit de sinistrali parte Britanniae ad regnum Cantorum et de ipso orti sunt reges Cantorum. Tunc Arthur pugnabat contra illos in illis diebus cum regibus Brittonum, sed ipse erat dux bellorum. Primum bellum fuit in ostium fluminis quod dicitur Glein. Secundum et tertium et quartum et quintum super aliud flumen, quod dicitur Dubglas et est in regione Linnuis. Sextum bellum super flumen, quod vocatur Bassas. Septimum fuit bellum in silva Celidonis, id est Cat Coit Celidon. Octavum fuit bellum in castello Guinnion, in quo Arthur portavit imaginem sanctae Mariae perpetuae virginis super humeros suos et pagani versi sunt in fugam in illo die et caedes magna fuit super illos per virtutem domini nostri Iesu Christi et per virtutem sanctae Mariae genetricis eius. Nonum bellum gestum est in urbe Legionis. Decimum gessit bellum in litore fluminis, quod vocatur Tribruit. Undecimum factum est bellum in monte, qui dicitur Agned. Duodecimum fuit bellum in monte Badonis, in quo corruerunt in uno die nongenti sexaginta viri de uno impetu Arthur; et nemo prostravit eos nisi ipse solus, et in omnibus bellis victor extitit.*

> [*Historia Brittonum*, 56]

Notes:

1. Hengisto – Hengist, king of the Saxons, succeeded by Octha
2. sinistrali parte – from the North; *ad regnum Cantorum* – the kingdom of Kent
3. Glein – possibly either of the Glen rivers in Northumberland and Lincolnshire respectively
4. Dubglas – 'the Douglas', possibly a river near Lincoln; *Linnuis* = *Lindum*, the Roman name for Lincoln
5. Bassas – possibly Cambuslang near Glasgow
6. Cat Coit Celidon – Old Welsh for 'the battle of the Caledonian Forest', an area roughly around the Scottish borders
7. Guinnion – not convincingly identified
8. super humeros suos – probably not 'on his shoulders', but 'on his shield',

a confusion resulting from a scribe misreading the Old Welsh *scuid*, 'shoulder' for *scuit*, 'shield'; it seems more plausible that Arthur went into battle with a cross drawn on his shield than actually carrying one over his shoulders. Gerald of Wales (for whom see below) records that: *in anteriori parte clipei sui Beatae Virginis imaginem interius, ut eam in conflictu prae oculis semper haberet, depingi fecerat*, 'on the rear of his shield he had caused to be painted in the centre the image of the Blessed Virgin, so that he should always have her in front of his eyes in battle

9. urbe Legionis – possibly Chester, sometimes described as *Caer Legion* (= *urbs Legionis*)

10. Tribruit – also known as *Tryfrwyd*, various locations from the Frew at Stirling to the Severn at Gloucester have been suggested

11. Agned – Edinburgh according to Geoffrey of Monmouth's account

12. monte Badonis – AD 516; the site is unknown but in Geoffrey of Monmouth it is Bath, *Caer Badd* (see also Chapter 2 for Bede's mention of the battle)

13. uno impetu Arthur – the Latin form is *Arturus*, but Nennius treats the name Arthur as indeclinable, so here 'by one attack *of* Arthur'.

3. THE MADNESS OF MERLIN (GEOFFREY OF MONMOUTH, *c*. 1100–*c*. 1155)

Written after his prose *Historia*, Geoffrey's lengthy poem *Vita Merlini* (in Classical hexameters) portrays a rather different Merlin than the one familiar from Arthurian lore. Here we encounter a figure much more like the Myrddin of Welsh legend, a war leader who goes mad and wanders the forest uttering complaints and prophecies, and telling, in conversation with the bard Taliesin, of past and future events. Here we witness the beginning of Merlin's madness in the aftermath of battle.

> Deplangitque viros nec cessat fundere fletus
> Pulveribus crines sparsit vestesque rescidit
> Et prostratus humi nunc hac illacque volutat.
> Solatur Peredurus eum proceresque ducesque,
> Nec vult solari nec verba precantia ferre.
> Iam tribus emensis defleverat ille diebus
> Respueratque cibos, tantus dolor usserat illum

> *Inde novas furias, cum tot tantisque querelis*
> *Aera complesset, cepit furtimque recedit*
> *Et fugit ad silvas, nec vult fugiendo videri,*
> *Ingrediturque nemus gaudetque latere sub ornis*
> *Miraturque feras pascentes gramina saltus;*
> *Nunc has insequitur, nunc cursu preterit illas.*
> *Utitur herbarum radicibus, utitur herbis,*
> *Utitur arboreo fructu morisque rubeti;*
> *Fit silvester homo quasi silvis deditus esset.*
> *Inde per estatem totam nullique repertus*
> *Oblitusque sui cognatorumque suorum*
> *Delituit silvis obductus more ferino.*
> *At cum venit hiems herbasque tulisset et omnes*
> *Arboreos fructus nec quo frueretur haberet*
> *Diffudit tales miseranda voce querelas:*
> *'Celi Christe Deus quid agam, qua parte morari*
> *Terrarum potero cum nil quo vescar adesse?'*.

[*Vita Merlini*, 65–88]

Notes:

1. Metre – hexameters, see Appendix
2. deplangitque viros – Merlin mourns for those who have fallen in battle; he is inconsolable (*nec vult solari*) despite the efforts of his companion Peredurus and his retinue (*Solatur Peredurus eum proceresque ducesque*)
3. emensis – participle from *emetior*, with *tribus diebus*: 'for three measured-out days', i.e. 'three whole days'
4. usserat – pluperfect of *uro*, 'burn, consume'
5. fugiendo – gerund, 'while fleeing'
6. sub ornis – 'beneath the ash-trees'
7. saltus – genitive singular, 'of the glade'
8. preterit – for *praeterit*; *cursu* – 'at a run'
9. utitur – 'consumes, eats' + ablative, hence *radicibus, herbis*; *arboreo fructu*, 'the fruit of the trees'; *moris rubeti*, 'the blackberries from the bramble bush'
10. estatem – for *aestatem*
11. obductus – participle from *obduco*, 'enclosed' or 'covered', i.e. he is clothed in animal hide
12. hiems – 'winter' is the subject of *tulisset*, Merlin the subject of *quo frueretur haberet*, 'he could not enjoy what he had'

13. miseranda voce – literally, 'with a voice to-be-pitied'

14. Celi – for *caeli*, genitive

15. vescar – 'since there is nothing here I can eat'; *vescar* takes the ablative, hence *quo*.

4. THE GREATNESS OF ARTHUR (JOSEPH OF EXETER, FL. 1184)

This short section from Joseph of Exeter's epic crusader poem *Antiocheis* is quoted in William Camden's *Britannia* (see *Annus Mirabilis*, Chapter 6); the poem is otherwise lost. Joseph sailed to the Holy Land during the Third Crusade (1189–92) and on his return home lionised King Richard I in verse. Here Joseph compares the kings and heroes of olden days, the greatest of whom was surely Arthur:

> *Hinc celebri fato foelici claruit ortu*
> *Flos regum Arthurus, cuius cum facta stupori,*
> *Non micuere minus, totus quod in aure voluptas,*
> *Et populo plaudente favus. Quemcumque priorum*
> *Inspice, Pelaeum commendat fama tyrannum,*
> *Pagina Caesareos loquitur Romana triumphos,*
> *Alcidem domitis attollit gloria monstris.*
> *Sed nec pinetum corili, nec sidera solem*
> *Aequant: annales Latios, Graiosque revolve,*
> *Prisca parem nescit, aequalem postera nullum*
> *Exhibitura dies. Reges supereminet omnes,*
> *Solus praeteritis melior, maiorque futuris.*

Notes:

1. Metre – hexameters, see Appendix

2. celebri … foelici – 'by distinguished good fortune'; *fato … ortu* – 'by destined birth'

3. micuere – abbreviated form of *micauerunt*, 'his deeds (*facta*) though astonishing (*cum stupori*) shone no less'

4. favus – 'in the people's applause (*populo plaudente*) he was wholly (*totus*) honey-sweet (*flavus*)'

5. Pelaeum – or *Pellaeum*, adjective referring to Alexander, who was born in the city of Pella

6.   Alcidem – adjective referring to Hercules, the grandson of Alcides, who subdued monsters (*domitis monstris*)

7.   Corili – for *coryli*, hazel trees

8.   prisca – 'the olden days'.

5. THE DEATH OF ARTHUR (GEOFFREY OF MONMOUTH, *c.*1100–*c.*1155)

In this account Geoffrey follows the ninth-century *Annales Cambriae* in placing Arthur's last battle at Camlann (AD 537, *in qua Arthur et Medraut corruerunt*). As with so many Arthurian sites the name remains a matter for much debate, with locations from Camelon in Scotland to the River Camel in Cornwall all being advanced as possible candidates. As we pick up the story, both Arthur and his villainous nephew Mordred are preparing their opposing armies for a final battle.

> *Ipsis itaque commilitones suos hinc et inde cohortantibus, subito impetu concurrunt acies, et commisso praelio crebros ictus innectere elaborabant. Fiunt ilico in utriusque partibus tantae strages, tanti morientium gemitus, tanti invadentium furores, quantos et dolorosum et laboriosum est describere. Undique etenim vulnerabant et vulnerabantur, perimebant perimebantur. Postquam autem multum diei in hunc modum duxerunt, irruit tandem Arturus cum agmine uno, quo sex milia sexcentos et sexaginta sex posuerat, in turmam illam ubi Modredum sciebat esse, et viam gladiis aperiendo, eam penetravit, atque tristissimam caedem ingessit. Concidit namque proditor ille nefandus, et multa milia cum eo. Nec tamen ob casum eius diffugiunt ceteri, sed ex omni campo confluentes, quantum audaciae dabatur, resistere conantur. Committitur ergo dirissima pugna inter eos, qua omnes fere duces qui in ambabus partibus affuerant, cum suis catervis corruerunt. Corruerunt etenim in parte Mordredi: Cheldricus, Elafius, Egbricius, Bunignus, Saxones; Gillapatriae, Gillamor, Gislafel, Gillarium, Hibernenses. Scoti etiam et Picti cum omnibus fere quibus deminabantur. In parte autem Arturi: Olbrictus rex Norwegiae, Aschillius rex Daciae, Cador Limenic, Cassibellanus, cum multis milibus suorum tam Britonum quam ceterarum gentium quas secum adduxerat. Sed et inclitus ille Arturus rex letaliter vulneratus est, qui illinc ad sananda vulnera sua in insulam Avallonis advectus, cognato suo Constantino, filio Cadoris ducis Cornubiae, diadema Britanniae concessit, anno ab incarnatione dominica quingentesimo quadragesimo secundo.*

[*Historia Regum Britanniae*, 11.2]

Notes:

1. hinc et inde cohortantibus – 'while the commanders on both sides were exhorting their men'

2. in turmam – 'against that squadron'

3. proditor ille nefandus – 'that execrable traitor', Mordred

4. quantum audaciae dabatur – literally, 'as much as was ascribed to their boldness', i.e. 'as far as their boldness allowed'

5. ambabus – *ambo* can be either regular *–is* in the dative/ablative plural or, as here, *–bus*

6. suis catervis – 'along with their own men'

7. tam Britonum quam ceterarum gentium – 'as many Britons as the other nations they had brought with them'

8. insulam Avallonis – the mysterious isle of Avalon, identified by Gerald of Wales (below) as Glastonbury

9. diadema – 'the crown of Britain'.

6. ARTHUR'S BONES (GERALD OF WALES, *c.*1146–*c.*1223)

Gerald of Wales (*Giraldus Cambrensis*) is best remembered for his *Itinerarium Cambriae*, a literary journey through Wales which provides much valuable historical and geographical information. But buried in one of his other books – a treatise on the education of a monarch, *De instructione principis* – is the story of how King Arthur's bones were discovered at Glastonbury in 1191 after Henry II, having heard tales of Arthur during his tour of Wales, ordered a search to be made for them.

It is hardly necessary to add that this discovery and the resulting publicity was particularly fortuitous for the monks whose Abbey had burnt down a few years earlier and

'The old monks were, when the fit took them, such very mendacious personages that one can hardly believe their tales implicitly. It is quite on the cards that they heard the report of the burial of Arthur in their "place of tombs", and determined that when his coffin was searched for it should be found. They were quite equal to scratching Roman letters on a stone lid, and filling an old oak chest with the bones of a deceased quadruped, which in those days of anatomical ignorance would pass muster very well as the bodily relics of "Uther's mythic son".'
Daily Telegraph, 29 August 1880

who were more than a little strapped for cash (in previous years these same monks had 'found' the bones of both St Patrick and St Dunstan). In 1278 the remains were transferred to a marble tomb in the Abbey Church, but disappeared during the dissolution of the monasteries.

Huius autem corpus, quod quasi phantasticum in fine, et tanquam per spiritus ad longinqua translatum, neque morti obnocium fabulae confinxerant, his nostris diebus apud Glastoniam inter lapideas pyramides duas, in coemiterio sacro quondam erectas, profundius in terra quercu concava reconditum, et signatum miris indiciis et quasi miraculosis, est inventum, et in ecclesiam cum honore translatum marmoreoque decenter tumulo commendatum. Unde et crux plumbea lapide supposito, non superius ut nostris solet diebus, sed inferiori potius ex parte infixa, quam nos quoque vidimus, namque tractavimus litteras has insculptas et non eminentes et exstantes, sed magis interius ad lapidem versas, continebat: 'Hic iacet sepultus inclitus rex Arthurus cum Wenneuereia uxore sua secunda in insula Avallonia.'

Occurrunt hic autem notabilia plurima; habuerat enim uxores duas, quarum ultima simul cum ipso sepulta fuerat, et ossa ipsius cum ossibus viri simul inventa, sic distincta tamen, ut duae partes sepulchri, versus caput scilicet, ossibus viri continendis deputatae fuissent, tertia vero versus pedes ossa muliebria seorsum contineret; ubi et trica comae muliebris flava cum integritate pristina et colore reperta fuit, quam ut monachus quidam avide manu arripuit et sublevavit, tota statim in pulverem decidit ...

Quae nunc autem Glastonia dicitur, antiquitus insula Avallonia dicebatur. Est enim quasi insula tota paludibus obsita, unde dicta est Britannice Inis Avallon, *id est, insula pomifera. Pomis enim, quae* aval *Britannica lingua dicuntur, locus ille quondam abundabat. Unde et Morganis, nobilis matrona et partium illarum dominatrix atque patrona, necnon et Arthuro regi sanguine propinqua, post bellum de Kemelen Arthurum ad sanandum eiusdem vulnera in insulam quae nunc Glastonia dicitur deportavit. Dicta quoque quondam Britannice* Inis gutrin *fuerat, hoc est, insula vitrea; ex quo vocabulo supervenientes postea Saxones locum illum* Glastingeburi *vocitabant.* Glas *enim lingua eorum vitrum sonat, et* buri *castrum, civitas appellatur.*

Sciendum etiam quod ossa reperta corporis Arthuri tam grandia fuerunt, ut et illud poetae completum in his videri posset:

'Grandiaque effossis mirabitur ossa sepulchris'

Os enim tibiae ipsius appositum tibiae longissimi viri loci, quem et nobis abbas ostendit, et iuxta pedem illius terrae affixum, large tribus digitis trans genu ipsius se porrexit. Os etiam capitis tanquam ad prodigium vel ostentum capax erat et grossum, adeo ut intercilium et inter oculos spatium palmalem amplitudinem large contineret. Apparebant autem in hoc vulnera decem aut plura, quae cuncta praeter unum maius caeteris, quod hiatum grandem fecerat, quodque solum letale fuisse videbatur, in solidam convenerant cicatricem.

[*De Instructione Principis, Distinctio* 1]

Notes:

1. corpus – Arthur's body, which so the tales had alleged (*fabulae confinxerant*) was like a phantasm and transferred to far-away places (*ad longinqua*) nor was it subject (*obnocium = obnoxium*) to death

2. pyramides – the tomb was found in the cemetery between two stone pyramids, deeply hidden (*profundius*) by a hollow oak

3. reconditum … signatum … inventum – all refer to the corpus

4. marmoreque … tumulo – the bones were moved to a marble tomb in the Abbey Church

5. crux plumbea – this lead cross was described in 1586 by William Camden in his *Britannia* (for which, see *Annus Mirabilis*, Chapter 6)

6. ossibus viri continendis – two thirds of the tomb had been assigned to contain the bones of Arthur; the woman's bones were placed near his feet

7. trica … flava – 'a blonde lock'

8. paludibus obsita – 'covered with marshes'

9. Morganis – Arthur's half-sister Morgana le Fay is in later versions an evil sorceress and Arthur's foe

10. bellum de Kemelen – the Battle of Camlann was traditionally Arthur's last; see Geoffrey of Monmouth above, though it is not mentioned by Nennius

11. sciendum – 'it must be known'

12. Grandiaque … sepulchris –Virgil, *Georgics* 1.497, the farmer marvelling at the bones of fallen warriors dug up by his plough

13. os enim tibiae – the shinbone was found to stand three fingers taller than the knee of the tallest man there

14. grossum – a late-Latin adjective, 'thick'; *intercilium* – the space between the eyebrows; *palmalem* – from *palmalis*, a late-Latin equivalent to *palmaris*, 'a hand's width'

15. in solidam … cicatricem – all the wounds had knitted together (*convenerant*) into a scar, except the largest one which seemed to have been lethal.

RECOMMENDED READING:

Geoffrey of Monmouth   *The History of the Kings of Briton*
(ed. Reeve)   Boydell Press

A new (2007) critical edition of the *Historia* with a facing-page English
translation by Neil Wright.

Geoffrey of Monmouth   *Vita Merlini*
(ed Parry)   Bibliobazaar/Forgotten Books

Reprint of John Jay Parry's 1925 Latin text and English translation.

Gerald of Wales   *Giraldi Cambrensis Opera, Vol.* 8
(ed Wright)   *(De instructione principis)*
                               Elibron Classics

A facsimile reprint of the 1891 edition.

Nennius (ed Morris)   *British History and The Welsh Annals*
                               Phillimore

Volume 8 of the Arthurian Period Sources series: Latin and English text.

CHAPTER 4

SAINTS AND MARTYRS

The veneration of saints and martyrs provided the early church with a subsitute for the pagan rites which it had so effectively suppressed by the early years of the fifth century. In his *Lives of the Sophists* (AD 405), the pagan scholar Eunapius rails against the Christians and their unworthy new objects of worship:

> The heads, salted and pickled, of those infamous malefactors, who for the multitude of their crimes have suffered a just and ignominious death; their bodies, still marked by the impression of the lash, and the scars of those tortures which were inflicted by the sentence of the magistrate; such are the gods which the earth produces in our days; such are the martyrs, the supreme arbitrators of our prayers and petitions to the Deity, whose tombs are now consecrated as the objects of the veneration of the people.
>
> [quoted in Gibbon, *Decline and Fall*, Chapter XXVIII]

Britain had its fair share of martyrs, the earliest being St Alban, whose martydom at the Roman town of Verulamium (modern St Albans) is related in Book I of Bede's *Historia Ecclesiastica*.

Saints inspired worship, too, both by the sanctity of their lives and by their oft-cited ability to perform miracles. Indeed, miracle-working at one time threatened to become so ubiquitous that, as Gibbon wryly remarks, the practice almost ceased to merit the description 'miraculous'.

Not surprising, therefore, that hagiography was a flourishing literary genre, both lives of individuals and collections such as the *Lives of the Saints* written by Aelfric of Eynsham (*c*.955–1010) for use on specific saints' days throughout the church year. Such saintly biographies are valuable literary texts, giving us both historical information and, more importantly, a window into the medieval mind.

'We may surely be allowed to observe, that a miracle, in that age of superstition and credulity, lost its name and its merit, since it could scarcely be considered as a deviation from the ordinary, and established, laws of nature.' [Gibbon, *Decline and Fall*, Chapter XXVIII]

1. THE MARTYDOM OF ST ALBAN (BEDE, *c*.672–735)

Alban was a native Romano-Briton who converted from paganism
to Christianity after providing shelter for a fugitive priest in his
house. When the Roman soldiers came to arrest the priest, Alban
is said to have exchanged his cloak with the cleric, allowing him to
escape in disguise while Alban was arrested and tried in his stead. He
was executed by beheading on the hill outside the walls of Roman
Verulamium where his cathedral now stands, behind which is the city
that now bears his name.

Bede places the death of Alban while *Diocletianus in oriente,
Maximianus Herculius in occidente*, 'Diocletian in the east, Maximian
in the west' were rulers of the Roman Empire, that is sometime in
the early years of the fourth century. But other sources place the
event earlier – the *Anglo-Saxon Chronicle* cites 283 – and some recent
scholars have argued for an even earlier date.

We pick up the action after Alban has been tried and condemned.
He is now being led to the place of execution:

> *Cumque ad mortem duceretur, pervenit ad flumen, quo murus ab harena, ubi
> feriendus erat, meatu rapidissimo dividebatur; viditque ibi non parvam hominum
> multitudinem utriusque sexus, condicionis diversae et aetatis, quae sine dubio
> divinitatis instinctu ad obsequium beatissimi confessoris ac martyris vocabatur, et ita
> fluminis ipsius occupabat pontem, ut intra vesperam transire vix posset. Denique
> cunctis paene egressis, iudex sine obsequio in civitate substiterat. Igitur sanctus
> Albanus, cui ardens inerat devotio mentis ad martyrium ocius pervenire, accessit ad
> torrentem, et dirigens ad caelum oculos, illico siccato alveo, vidit undam suis cessisse ac
> viam dedisse vestigiis. Quod cum inter alios etiam ipse carnifex, qui eum percussurus
> erat, vidisset, festinavit ei, ubi ad locum destinatum morti venerat, occurrere, divino
> nimirum admonitus instinctu, proiectoque ense, quem strictum tenuerat, pedibus
> eius advolvitur, multum desiderans, ut cum martyre, vel pro martyre, quem percutere
> iubebatur, ipse potius mereretur percuti.*
>
> *Dum ergo is ex persecutore factus esset collega veritatis et fidei, ac iacente ferro
> esset inter carnifices iusta cunctatio, montem cum turbis reverentissimus Dei confessor
> ascendit; qui opportune laetus, gratia decentissima, quingentis fere passibus ab harena
> situs est, variis herbarum floribus depictus, immo usquequaque vestitus; in quo
> nihil repente arduum, nihil praeceps, nihil abruptum, quem lateribus longe lateque
> deductum in modum aequoris natura complanat, dignum videlicet eum, pro insita sibi
> specie venustatis, iam olim reddens, qui beati martyris cruore dicaretur In huius ergo*

vertice sanctus Albanus dari sibi a Deo aquam rogavit, statimque, incluso meatu, ante pedes eius fons perennis exortus est, ut omnes agnoscerent etiam torrentem martyri obsequium detulisse, neque enim fieri poterat, ut in arduo montis cacumine martyr aquam, quam in fluvio non reliquerat, peteret, si hoc opportunum esse non videret. Qui videlicet fluvius ministerio persoluto, devotione completa, officii testimonium relinquens reversus est ad naturam.

Decollatus itaque martyr fortissimus ibidem accepit coronam vitae, quam repromisit Deus diligentibus se. Sed ille, qui piis cervicibus impias intulit manus, gaudere super mortuum non est permissus; namque oculi eius in terram una cum beati martyris capite deciderunt. Decollatus est ibi etiam tum miles ille, qui antea superno nutu correptus, sanctum Dei confessorem ferire recusavit; de quo nimirum constat, quia, etsi fonte baptismatis non est ablutus, sui tamen est sanguinis lavacro mundatus, ac regni caelestis dignus factus ingressu.

[*Historia Ecclesiastica*, 1.7]

Notes:

1. cumque … duceretur – 'while he was being led'; imperfect subjunctive because, in the historic tense sequence (used for narrative), a perfect main verb requires a subjunctive verb in the *cum*-clause
2. murus – here meaning a 'walled settlement', i.e. the town
3. harena – a sandy arena was the place where gladiators fought; Bede here means the place of execution (*feriendus erat*)
4. condicionis diversae – 'of varying circumstance', i.e. people from all walks of life
5. divinitatis instinctu ad obsequium – 'the crowd was called (*vocabatur*) by a divine prompting (*divinitatis instinctu*) to escort (*ad obsequium*) the blessed confessor and martyr'; *ad obsequium*, literally 'to the attendance of …' hence genitive *beatissimi confessoris*
6. intra vesperam – 'within the space of that evening', i.e. the vast crowd so filled the bridge that it took a long time for them all to cross over;
7. iudex sine obsequio in civitate substiterat – the judge who had passed sentence on Alban was left in the city without any escort (*sine obsequio*); *substiterat* – pluperfect, 'had remained'
8. cui … inerat – *insum* is intransitive, hence dative *cui*; since Alban was possessed by a burning desire to attain martyrdom *ocius* (comparative, 'more swiftly'), and since he can't get across the crowded bridge, he decides to cross the river by a more direct route
9. siccato alveo – ablative absolute, 'with the river channel (*alveus*) having dried up'

10. undam ... cessisse – accusative + infinitive after *vidit*: 'that the flow had ceased'; *suis ... viam dedisse vestigiis* – 'that a path had been given to his footsteps'

11. percussurus erat – the executioner (*carnifex*) who was going to kill him saw this miracle and, prompted by divine instigation (*divino admonitus instinctu*), flings his drawn sword (*strictum*, participle from *stringo*) and himself at the martyr's feet, begging to be executed in his stead

12. collega – the executioner became Alban's colleague, while the other *carnifices* hesitated to pick up his sword which was lying on the ground

13. opportune laetus, gratia decentissima – the hill (where the cathedral now stands) was a pleasant and agreeable spot

14. variis herbarum floribus depictus – a description of the hill, which is painted (*depictus*) or rather clothed (*vestitus*) in flowers; it is not difficult (*arduum*), precipitous (*praeceps*) or steep (*abruptum*); nature levels off (*complanat*) its sides, sloping away in all directions (*longe lateque*), in the manner of a plain

15. pro insita sibi specie venustatis – 'by its innate appearance of beauty'; *iam olim reddens* – 'for a long time past reappearing'

16. dicaretur – 'to be consecrated

17. Albanus ... aquam rogavit – he asks God to give him water, and a spring appears at his feet

18. torrentem martyri obsequium detulisse – accusative + infinitive, 'that the river flowed in compliance with the wish of the martyr'

19. fieri poterat ut – 'it was not possible that ...'

20. aquam, quam in fluvio non reliquerat, peteret – having left the river below dry, he would not have sought water on the dry summit unless he saw that it was advantageous (*si hoc opportunum esse non videret*) – that is, it was time for another miracle

21. officii testimonium relinquens – the river leaves behind a testimony of its obligation to Alban before returning to its original state (*ad naturam*)

22. decollatus – 'having been beheaded', the actual execution is passed over

23. repromisit – 'which God guarantees to those who love him'

24. piis cervicibus – plural presumably referring poetically to Alban's (singular) neck

25. una cum beati martyris capite – the executioner's eyes fall to the ground at the same time (*una*) as Alban's head!

26. miles ille – the *carnifex* who had thrown his sword at Alban's feet

27. superno nutu correptus – literally, 'carried away by a divine nod of assent', i.e. warned by a heavenly sign

28. constat – 'it is agreed'

29. mundatus – from *mundare*, 'he was cleansed (i.e. his sins were removed as in baptism) by the spilling (*lavacro*, literally 'washing') of his own blood', hence he was deemed worthy to enter the kingdom of heaven.

2. A SAINT'S EARLY LIFE (ST PATRICK, *c.*390–461/493?)

Patrick was born into a wealthy Romano-British family, but while still a teenager he was kidnapped and carried across to Ireland where he was sold as a slave and remained for six years working as a herdsman. He eventually escaped captivity and returned home – but then experienced a vision which told him to return to Ireland and liberate its people from paganism. After receiving holy orders and perhaps even travelling to Rome he did just that in around 432. Although he doesn't seem to have banished any snakes from Ireland, he did convert many thousands to the new religion and thus became one of Christianity's first missionaries.

Two works ascribed to Patrick himself survive – an *Epistola ad Coroticum* and the *Confessio*, the latter written in old age contains his own account of his early life.

Confessio in epistola ad Hibernos explicata

Ego Patricius, peccator rusticissimus et minimus omnium fidelium et contemptibilis sum apud plurimos, patrem habui Calpornum diaconum filium quendam Potiti, filii Odissi presbyteri, qui fuit in vico Bannavem Taberniae. Villulam enim prope habuit, ubi ego capturam dedi. Annorum eram tunc fere sedecim. Deum verum ignorabam, et Hiberione in captivitate adductus sum, cum tot milia hominum, secundum merita nostra, quia a Deo recessimus, et praecepta eius non custodivimus, et sacerdotibus nostris non oboedientes fuimus, qui nostram salutem admonebant. Et Dominus induxit super nos iram animationis suae, et dispersit nos in gentibus multis, etiam usque ad ultimum terrae, ubi nunc parvitas mea esse videtur inter alienigenas. Et ibi Dominus aperuit sensum incredulitatis meae, ut vel sero rememorarem dilicta mea, ut converterem toto corde ad Dominum meum, qui respexit humilitatem meam et misertus est adolescentiae et ignorantiae meae, et custodivit me, antequam scirem eum, et antequam saperem vel distinguerem inter bonum et malum, et munivit me, et consulatus est mei, ut pater filium.

[*Confessio* 1]

Notes:

1. ad Hibernos explicata – his confession given to the Irish
2. diaconum – his father Calpornus was a deacon, son of Potitus son of Odissus
3. Bannavem Taberniae – the exact location is disputed, various theories identify it with Dumbarton in Scotland, Carlisle in Cumbria, Banwell in Somersetshire, or even Anglesey
4. villulam – a country residence nearby (*prope*)
5. capturam dedi – an odd expression (*captura* = game caught in a bag by a hunter), 'I was taken captive'
6. secundum merita nostra – 'deservedly so'
7. parvitas – 'my humble self'
8. alienigenas – 'foreigners'; even as an old man Patrick feels he is still a foreigner in Ireland
9. sensum incredulitatis meae – 'the consciousness of my disbelief'
10. rememorarem – from late-Latin *rememoror*, 'so that I might remember'; *dilicta* = *delicta*, 'my faults/crimes'
11. misertus est – perfect tense of *misereor*, 'have pity on', followed by datives *adolescentiae, ignorantiae*
12. consulatus – literally 'he is the consul of me', i.e. 'he counsels me'.

3. ST COLUMBA VS. THE 'LOCH NESS MONSTER' (ST ADAMNAN, *c*.624–704)

Saint Columba (or Columcille, 521–597) was an Irish missionary who travelled to Scotland after falling out with a fellow Irish saint (St Finnian), finally founding a monastic community on the Isle of Iona which he used as a base for converting the native Picts to Christianity. This he achieved via a series of miracles chronicled by his biographer Adamnan (or Adomnán or Eunan), who was Abbot of Iona as well as the Columban monasteries in Ireland and who was himself later canonised.

In this extract, Adamnan relates how Columba came to the River Ness, where a certain 'aquatic monster' was terrorising the locals.

De Cuiusdam Aquatilis Bestiae Virtute Orationis Beati Viri Repulsione

Alio quoque in tempore, cum vir beatus in Pictorum provinicia per aliquot moraretur dies, necesse habuit fluvium transire Nessam: ad cuius cum accessisset ripam, alios

ex accolis aspicit misellum humantes homunculum; quem, ut ipsi sepultores ferebant,
quaedam paulo ante nantem aquatilis praeripiens bestia morsu momordit saevissimo;
cuius miserum cadaver, sero licet, quidam in alno subvenientes porrectis praeripuere
uncinis. Vir e contra beatus, haec audiens, praecipit ut aliquis ex comitibus enatans,
caupallum, in altera stantem ripa, ad se navigando reducat. Quo sancti audito
praedicabilis viri praecepto, Lugneus Mocumin, nihil moratus, obsecundans, depositis
excepta vestimentis tunica, immittit se in aquas. Sed bellua, quae prius non tam
satiata, quam in praedam accensa, in profundo fluminis latitabat, sentiens eo nante
turbatam supra aquam, subito emergens, natatilis ad hominem in medio natantem
alveo, cum ingenti fremitu, aperto cucurrit ore. Vir tum beatus videns, omnibus qui
inerant, tam barbaris quam etiam fratribus, nimio terrore perculsis, cum salutare,
sancta elevata manu, in vacuo aere crucis pinxisset signum, invocato Dei nomine,
feroci imperavit bestiae dicens, Noles ultra progredi, nec hominem tangas; retro citius
revertere. Tum vero bestia, hac Sancti audita voce, retrorsum, ac si funibus retraheretur,
velociori recursu fugit tremefacta: quae prius Lugneo nanti eo usque appropinquavit,
ut hominem inter et bestiam non amplius esset quam unius contuli longitudo.
Fratres tum, recessise videntes bestiam, Lugneumque commilitonem ad eos intactum
et incolumen in navicula reversum, cum ingenti admiratione glorificaverunt Deum
in beato viro. Sed et gentiles barbari, qui ad praesens inerant, eiusdem miraculi
magnitudine, quod et ipsi viderant, compulsi, Deum magnificaverunt Christianorum.

[*Vita Sancti Columbae*, II.27]

Notes:

1. repulsione – after *de*
2. vir beatus – 'Saint'
3. Nessam – the River Ness flows out of Loch Ness through Inverness and empties into the Moray Firth
4. humantes – some of the locals (*alios ex accolis*) were burying (*humo, humare*) a wretched little man (*misellum homunculum*)
5. ferebant – the burial party tells the story
6. praeripiens – the present participle is sometimes used in Medieval Latin, as sometimes in English, to express an action completed before the main verb (*momordit*): 'snatching the man, the beast bit him'
7. sero licet – 'although too late'
8. alno – from *alnus cavata*, literally 'hollowed out alder-wood', i.e. 'a boat'; the phrase occurs in Virgil; *porrectis uncinis* – 'with hooks which they held out'
9. e contra – 'on the contrary'
10. caupallum – *caupulus*, a small boat

11. enatans – present participle to express purpose: 'to swim out'

12. navigando – ablative gerund with *ut … reducat*: 'to sail back to him'

13. Lugneus Mocumin – one of Columba's followers, whom the Saint (in one of his lesser miracles to be sure) had once cured of a persistent nosebleed

14. satiata … accensa – 'not so much sated as aroused'

15. natatilis – a marine creature

16. cum salutare – he makes the sign of the cross with his index finger

17. revertere – imperative from deponent *revertor*

18. velociori recursu – 'with a speedier retreat'

19. contuli – 'the width of one little pole'; this diminutive of *contus*, 'a pole, pike', occurs uniquely here

20. navicula – 'a little boat'; Lugneus returns unharmed.

4. THE TRANSLATION OF ST CUTHBERT (SIMEON OF DURHAM, D. AFTER 1129)

After St Cuthbert died in 687 his remains were kept at Lindisfarne monastery until the Danes stormed the island in 875; the saint was moved to several other sites, ultimately to reside at Durham. In 1104 when a magnificent new cathedral was built there, Cuthbert's relics were 'translated' (from *transfero*, *translatum*) to a new shrine behind the altar. This was the second time the saint's casket had been opened (the first was just 11 years after his death) and his body found to be incorruptible. Such incorruptibility was probably an example of saponification ('soap-making') – a postmortem change in the fatty tissues into a waxy substance called adipocere, which preserves the body – but for the monks of Lindisfarne and Durham it was nothing less than a miracle. (As we shall see in Chapter 5, when non-saintly corpses remained intact, they tended to inspire fear rather than veneration.)

Simeon (or Symeon) was precentor of Durham priory who wrote several books about the history of the Durham monastic community in particular and northern English history in general. He tells the story of the opening of Cuthbert's tomb in his account of the 'translation' which begins,

Quomodo post cccc.x et viij annos corpus beati Cuthberti incorruptum sit inventum, et in novam ecclesiam translatum

As we join the action, the monks of Durham have moved the casket containing the saint's remains into the choir, but they are afraid to open it.

Ibi, ablato quod locellum obtexerat velamine, non statim ausi sunt aperire, sed cum candelis circumeuntes, diligenter explorarunt, si per aliquas forte rimulas vel aliud quodlibet indicium, quid intrinsecus lateret deprehendere potuissent. Sed cum haec agentibus nil certum pateret, tandem amoto, licet paventes, operculo, vident librum Evangeliorum ad caput supra tabulam positum … Tabulam quandoque levant, ablatoque quod proxime post tabulam sacras cooperuerat reliquias lintheamine, suavissimi odoris fragrantiam naribus trahunt. Et, ecce! beati patris venerabile corpus, scilicet fructum desiderii sui, reperiunt, quod, in dextro latere iacens, tota sui integritate artuumque flexibilitate dormientem magis repraesentabat quam mortuum. Quo viso, pavore percelluntur ingenti, et paulo longius recedentes, non ausi sunt quod patebat intueri miraculum. Coeperunt flexis crebro genibus pectora pugnis tundere, et, oculis cum manibus in altum levatis, saepius inclamare, 'Miserere nostri, Domine, miserere.' Interdum id quod singuli viderant, ac si non vidissent, sibi vicissim nuntiare. Prostrati toto tandem corpore, lacrimis ubertim fluentibus, septem Poenitentialibus Psalmis supplicant Dominum, ne in furore Suo eos argueret, neque in ira Sua illos corriperet. Quibus finitis, genibus ac manibus potius reptando quam pedibus incedendo accedentes, tot Sanctorum reliquias ibidem conspiciunt, ut eas illius loculi angustia capere non potuisset, nisi sanctum patris corpus in latus, ut dictum est, decumbens, largius eis una secum quiescendi spatium hinc et inde permitteret. Quas profecto reliquias, ut in veteribus libris legitur, constat esse caput gloriosi regis et martyris Oswaldi, ossa quoque venerabilium confessorum Christi ac sacerdotum, Aidani videlicet, et successorum ipsius venerandi patris Cuthberti, scilicet Eadberti, Eadfridi, et Ethelwoldi. Praeterea et ossa Venerabilis Bedae, qui Vitam beati Cuthberti dilucide conscripserat, una cum illius corpore hospitium quietis habuerant, quae pariter continebat sacculus de lino … Aliorum quoque Sanctorum plurimae ibidem reliquae sunt repertae.

[*Historia Translationum Sancti Cuthberti*]

Notes:

1. post cccc.x et viij annos – Cuthbert died in 687, so these events took place in 1104
2. ablato … velamine – they removed the outer covering which had concealed the actual casket (*locellum*)
3. agentibus – those who were inspecting the casket for cracks or other indications of what was inside

4. amoto … operculo – they removed the lid

5. librum Evangeliorum – the Stonyhurst Gospel, dating from the seventh century, now in the British Museum

6. ablato … lintheamine – the linen cloth which covered the remains; *reliquias* – 'relics'

7. tota sui integritate – his body remained incorrupted

8. quod patebat – 'they didn't dare to gaze on the miracle which was revealed'

9. septem Poenitentialibus Psalmis – that is, Psalms 6, 31, 37, 50, 101, 129 and 142

10. ne in furore Suo .. in ira Sua illos corriperet – Psalm 6, *Domine, ne in furore tuo arguas me, neque in ira tua corripias me*, 'O Lord, rebuke me not in thine anger, neither chasten me in thy hot displeasure' (King James version)

11. reptando – they approach on hands and knees

12. capere non potuisset – 'the narrowness of the casket would not have been able to hold them'

13. in latus – 'to one side'; Cuthbert's body is on its side in order to accommodate all the other relics *hinc et inde* – 'here and there'

14. constat esse – 'it is agreed that those relics are …'

15. Oswaldi … Aidani – St Oswald (*c.*604–642) was a Northumbrian king who spread Christianity throughout the region; St Aidan (d. 651) founded the monastery at Lindisfarne

16. Bedae – the bones of the Venerable Bede (Chapter 2) had been placed in Cuthbert's original tomb some decades earlier; they were reburied in the Galilee Chapel

17. una cum illius corpore – 'along with his body had occupied this place of rest'

18. sacculus de lino – a linen sack.

5. THE MARTYRDOM OF BECKET (EDWARD GRIM, FL. 1180)

King Henry II and his Lord Chancellor Thomas Becket (or Thomas à Becket) were on terms of great intimacy, and Becket at first supported the king in his bid to establish himself as the supreme power in the land. But when Becket was made Archbishop of Canterbury in 1162 a great change occurred – he resigned as Lord Chancellor and began actively to champion the prerogative of the Church, exerting his influence in opposition to the king's decrees and even threatening the excommunication of the king himself. On hearing of Becket's continuing disobedience, Henry is said to have exclaimed (according to Edward Grim):

'*Inertes ac miseros homines enutrivi et erexi in regno meo, qui nec fidem ferunt domino suo, quem a plebeo quodam clerico tam probrose patiuntur illudi.*'

'I have nurtured and raised useless and contemptible men in my kingdom, who show no loyalty to their master, whom they allow to be trifled with so basely by a low-born cleric.'

Taking these words as a positive call to arms, four of Henry's retinue – Hugh de Moreville, William de Tracy, Richard le Breton (or Brito) and Reginald FitzUrse – set out for Canterbury intending to murder the 'troublesome priest'.

Edward Grim, a monk from Cambridge, was with Becket on Tuesday 29 December 1170, as the four knights entered the cathedral with drawn swords. Grim attempted to shield the Archbishop from the blows and was himself wounded on the arm. In his later biography of the man who was now a saint (he was canonised in 1173), Grim recalls the events of that day. We join his account as Becket (the *invictus martyr*) realises (*cernens*) that his final hour has come:

Cernens martyr invictus horam imminere quae miserae mortalitati finem imponeret, paratam sibi et promissam a Domino coronam immortalitatis iam proximam fieri, inclinata in modum orantis cervice, iunctis pariter et elevatis sursum manibus, Deo et sanctae Mariae et beato martyri Dionysio suam et ecclesiae causam commendavit.

*Vix verbum implevit, et metuens nefandus miles ne raperetur a populo et vivus evaderet, insiliit in eum subito, et summitate coronae, quam sancti chrismatis unctio dicaverat Deo, abrasa, agnum Deo immolandum vulneravit in capite, eodem ictu praeciso brachio haec referentis. Is etenim, fugientibus tam monachis quam clericis universis, sancto archiepiscopo constanter adhaesit, et inter ulnas complexum tenuit, donec ipsa quam opposuit praecisa est. … Deinde alio ictu in capite recepto adhuc quoque permansit immobilis. Tertio vero percussus martyr genua flexit et cubitos, seipsum hostiam viventem offerendo, dicens submissa voce, '*Pro nomine Iesu et ecclesiae tuitione mortem amplecti paratus sum.*' At tertius miles ita procumbenti grave vulnus inflixit, quo ictu et gladium collisit lapidi, et coronam, quae ampla* *fuit, ita a capite separavit, ut sanguis albens ex cerebro, cerebrum nihilominus rubens ex sanguine, lilii et rosae coloribus virginis et matris ecclesiae faciem confessoris et martyris vita et morte purpuraret. Quartus miles supervenientes abegit ut caeteri liberius ac licentius homicidium perpetrarent. Quintus vero, non miles, sed clericus ille qui cum militibus intraverat, ne martyri Quinta plaga deesset, qui in aliis Christum fuerat imitatus, posito pede super collum sancti sacerdotis et martyris pretiosi (horrendum dictu) cerebrum cum sanguine per pavimentum spargens caeteris exclamavit, 'Abeamus hinc, milites, iste ulterius non resurget.'*

'This was the tragical end of Thomas à Becket, a prelate of the most lofty, intrepid, and inflexible spirit, who was able to cover to the world, and probably to himself, the enterprises of pride and ambition under the disguise of sanctity and of zeal for the interests of religion.' David Hume, *History of England*

Sed in his omnibus incredibilis constantiae virtutem exhibens martyr insignis nec manum nec vestem, ut est infirmitatis humanae, opposuit percussori, nec percussus verbum protulit, nec clamorem edidit, non gemitum, non sonum cuiscunque doloris indicem; sed caput quod inclinaverat gladiis evaginatis immobile tenuit, donec confusus sanguine et cerebro, tanquam ad orandum pronus, in pavimento corpus, in sinum Abrahae spiritum collocavit.

[*Vita Sanctae Thomae, Cantuariensis Archepiscopi et Martyris,* 81–3]

Notes:

1. horam imminere … coronam fieri – accusatives + infinitives after *cernens*
2. inclinata … cervice – ablative absolute
3. Dionysio – either Dionysius the Areopagite, who was martyred in AD 96 A.D., or Denis Bishop of Paris, martyred c.250, both of whom were beheaded
4. nefandus miles – Reginald FitzUrse delivered the first blow to the top of Becket's shaved head (*summitate … abrasa*), which had been anointed with the holy oil *chrism* (myrrh)
5. agnum … immolandum – 'the lamb being sacrificed to God'
6. eodem ictu praeciso brachio haec referentis – 'with the arm of he who is relating this having been maimed by the same blow', Grim himself was wounded defending Becket; *is etenim* refers to Grim, who stayed behind while all the other monks and priests fled (*fugientibus tam monachis quam clericis universis*)
7. deinde – I have omitted a parenthetical exclamation about the saint's worthiness

8. tertio vero percussus – William de Tracy struck the third blow

9. genua flexit et cubitos – 'bent his knees and elbows'

10. offerendo – 'while he offered himself as a living sacrifice'

11. tertius miles – Richard le Breton's blow was so hard that he severed the large (*ampla*) crown of Becket's head and his sword then struck the stone pavement and broke

12. ut sanguis … purpuraret – 'so that the blood … stained the appearance of the church (*faciem ecclesiae*) with the colours of the lily and the rose, the colours of the virgin and mother, with the life and death of the confessor and martyr'

13. clericus ille – Hugh of Horsea (aka Mauclerc), chaplain of nearby Saltwood Castle, who had entered the cathedral with the four knights

14. ne martyri Quinta plaga deesset – Becket should suffer five wounds like Christ on the cross

15. in his omnibus – 'while all this was going on'

16. percussori – 'to the assassin'

17. gladiis evaginatis – 'to the roaming swords'

18. confusus – 'suffused (with)'

19. ad orandum – *ad* + gerundive to indicate purpose.

RECOMMENDED READING:

St Patrick (trans. Skinner) *Confession and Letter to Coroticus*
Bantam Doubleday and Dell

Adamnan (trans. Sharpe) *Life of St Columba*
Penguin Classics

CHAPTER 5

FROM SUPERSTITION TO SCIENCE

The medieval period is often characterised as an age of superstition when even the most serious of scholars believed in all kinds of supernatural phenomena – we have already seen that saints were said to perform miracles and remain miraculously incorruptible after death. That the situation was not quite so clear cut may become evident from the following extracts, in which men of learning make honest attempts to understand their world. And before we condemn their age as backward, reflect for a moment that the situation hardly seems to have improved today even in societies that have supposedly experienced a cultural Renaissance and a scientific Age of Enlightenment. People who still read horoscopes in daily newspapers, believe in the healing power of crystals, or embrace fundamentalist Creation 'science' should not rush to judge those who wrote credulously about vampires or the man in the moon.

1. A MEDIEVAL VAMPIRE (WALTER MAP, *c*.1140–*c*.1208/10)

In pre-industrial societies the often disturbing phenomena associated with death and decomposition gave rise to a remarkable body of folklore concerning revenants (that is corpses who have returned from the grave). Our modern concept of the vampire (from the Slavic word *vampir*) – the urbane gentleman of Bram Stoker's novel – is rather different from that envisaged by the people of medieval Britain: for them, any corpse that seemed to have miraculously dug itself up or shown signs of movement after death was a revenant. But as is now better understood, the body after death undergoes numerous changes: it swells up, hair and nails appear to grow, teeth protrude from retreating gums, coagulated blood can re-liquify and be forced out of the nose and mouth by the build up of gasses in the abdomen and so on, *ad nauseam* (literally). Forces such as erosion, flooding and the activities of nocturnal scavengers could cause corpses to 'return' from poorly dug shallow graves and be labelled as revenants.

Walter Map (*Gualteri Mapes*) was both a friend of Thomas Becket (Chapter 4) and an intimate of King Henry II who held various ecclesiastical posts, ultimately becoming Archdeacon of Oxford. He apparently compiled his entertaining collection of gossip, trivia, folklore and satire known as *De Nugis Curialium*, 'Courtiers' Trifles', over a period of several years. The work is divided into five parts known as *Distinctiones* ('divisions'), in the second of which Map recounts several folkloric tales mostly from Welsh sources (Map was probably from Herefordshire or Gloucestershire). In this passage he tells of a disturbing event that occurred in a Welsh village during the time when Gilbert Foliot was Bishop of Hereford (1149–1162).

'People often have found many reasons to "kill" or inactivate a corpse ... these methods often aimed quite specifically at preventing certain acts of vampires believed, on the basis of observations of corpses, to be their typical behaviour. The tongue protrudes and blood seeps from the open mouth; therefore the vampire must attack his victims with teeth or tongue and suck their blood. Logically enough, the people retaliate by attacking its mouth or head.' Paul Barber, *Vampires, Burial and Death* (Yale)

De quodam prodigio

Maximum scio contigisse in Wallia prodigium. Willelmus Laudun, miles Anglicus, fortis viribus et audaciae probatae, venit ad Gillebertum Foliot, tunc episcopum Herefordensum, nunc autem Lundoniensem, dicens, 'Domine, ad te confugio consilium petens: quidam maleficus Walensis decessit satis nuper infideliter in villa mea, qui statim post quatuor noctes singulis ad villam noctibus repedans, non cessat evocare singillatim et nominatim convicaneos suos, qui statim vocati infirmantur et infra triduam moriuntur, ut iam pauci supersint.' Episcopus admirans ait, 'Potestatem forsitan dedit Dominus angelo illius perditi malo, ut in corpore illo mortuo se exagitet. Attamen effodiatur corpus illud, et collo reciso fossorio conspergatur ipsum et fossa magna aqua benedicta, et reponatur.' Cumque hoc fieret nihilominus errore pristino fatigati sunt ab eo residui. Nocte igitur quadam cum iam paucos reliquisset superstites, ipsum Willelmum trina citatione vocavit. At ille, ut erat animosus et impiger, non ignarus quid esset, nudato prosilit ense, fugientemque daemonem ad fossam usque secutus, ibi iam in fossa recidentem percussit in caput collo tenus, cessavitque ab illa hora persecutio pestis erraticae, nec ipsi Willelmo nec alicui aliorum exinde nocuit. Huius rei verum tenorum scimus, causam nescimus.

[*De Nugis Curialium, Distinctio Secunda*, 27]

Notes:

1. maximum ... prodigium – accusative + infinitive after *scio*, 'I know/ am aware that a very notable prodigy occurred'; *Wallia* – Wales

2. viribus – ablative of description, 'strong with/in respect of courage'

3. Gillebertum – Gilbert Foliot, Bishop of Hereford 1149–1162, then London 1163–87; an indication that this story was written before 1187

4. Walensis – 'Welshman'

5. satis .. infideliter – 'quite without faith'

6. singulis ...noctibus – 'on each successive night'

7. convicaneos suos – 'his fellow villagers'

8. angelo illius perditi malo – 'to an evil angel of the fall'; an *angelus perditus* is a fallen angel; *exagitet* – subjunctive after *ut*, 'to rouse itself'

9. fossorio – from the Late-Latin *fossorius*, a digging tool, i.e. a spade

10. errore pristino – 'by its former wandering'; the remaining villagers (*residui*) continued to be harrassed (*fatigati*)

11. trina citatione – 'with a triple invocation', the revenant summons William himself

12. quid esset – subjunctive in an indirect question: William knew what it was but still bravely pursued it; *nudato ... ense* – 'with sword drawn'

13. collo tenus – 'right up to the neck', i.e. he decapitated it while it was in the act of returning (*recidentem*) to the grave

14. pestis erraticae – 'the wandering plague/pest', i.e. the revenant

15. verum tenorum – 'the true tenor', Map says he knows the events actually happened as related, but admits he doesn't know the cause.

2. A LUNATIC THEORY (ALEXANDER NECKAM, 1157–1217)

Alexander Neckam (or Neckham or Nequam) was a distinguished scholar and teacher, Master of St Albans School and Abbot of Cirencester Abbey. He wrote treatises on theology and grammar as well as tackling natural history in his *De naturis rerum*. In this book he described the natural world not as an object of scientific study in its own right but as a vehicle for theological and moral speculation about man's place in the world. In passing he provides the first mention of a magnetic ship's compass being used in Europe (Book 2, Chapter 98). He also speculates on certain natural phenomena and provides moralistic explanations for them, such as this one for why the moon appears to have stains on its surface in the shape of a man's face.

De macula lunae

Nonnulli sollicitantur unde umbratilis quaedam macula in luna videatur. Placuit ergo quibusdam lunare corpus esse cavernosum, ita quod cavernae lunae lucis solaris radios in se non admittant. Aliis visum est corpus lunae non esse rotundum, sed in quibusdam sui partibus esse eminentius, in aliis depressius. Partes igitur depressae in modum convallium, beneficium lucis solaris non sentiunt. Haec autem opinio praedictae opinioni collimitanea est. Volunt alii lunare corpus in sui natura obscurum esse, ita ut quaedam eius partes obscuriores naturaliter sint aliis, unde et illuminationi non sunt obnoxiae. Sed sciendum est, in signum et in instructionem nostri hoc factum esse. Merito enim praevaricationis primorum parentum, omnium planetarum et stellarum fulgor dispendium claritatis sustinuit. Luna vero, quae vicina terris est, et aspectibus humanis familiarius occurrens, maculam in se detinuit, ad denotandum quod quamdiu in statu vitae praesentis currimus, macula aliqua in sancta ecclesia est. Cum autem omnes planetae cum stellis etiam stabunt quasi emeriti, stabilis erit status noster, et non erit aliqua macula in luna materiali, sicut nec in sancta ecclesisa. Forsitan simplex lector non advertit quid vocem lunae maculam. Nonne novisti quid vulgus vocet rusticum in luna portantem spinas? Unde quidam vulgariter loquens ait:

> *Rusticus in luna, quem sarcina deprimit una,*
> *Monstrat per spinas nulli prodesse rapinas.*

Quotiens igitur umbram illam dispersam conspicis, revoca ad memoriam transgressionem primorum parentum, et ingemisce. Postmodum vero te ipsum per spem erige, et suspira ad gloriam illius status in quo corpora glorificata clariora erunt sole, qui sicut et caeteri planetae cum stellis longe clarior erit quam modo sit. Quam felix erit coniunctio corporis et animae, quae multo erunt clariora sole? O claritas inenarrabilis, o claritas desiderabilis, o pulcritudo admirabilis.

[*De Naturis Rerum*, 1.14]

Notes:

1. sollicitantur – 'are investigating'
2. placuit … quibusdam – 'certain people are of the opinion', followed by accusative + infinitive
3. quod … admittant – equivalent to *ut* + subjunctive

4.   collimitanea – 'this opinion is bordering on the aforementioned', i.e. it amounts to the same thing

5.   volunt alii – 'others propose that …'

6.   obnoxiae – 'not subject to illumination'

7.   sciendum est – gerundive of obligation

8.   merito … praevaricationis – 'as a consequence of the transgression'; *dispendium claritatis* – 'a loss of brightness'

9.   familiarius occurrens – 'most familiarly occurring to human sight'

10.   ad denotandum – *ad* + gerund indicating purpose; *quod* – 'that'

11.   quasi emeriti – 'as if having discharged their duties'

12.   vocem … vocet – subjunctives in indirect questions, 'what I call … what he calls …'; *simplex* – naïve

13.   spinas – thorns, presumably a bundle of twigs

14.   rusticus … rapinas – a hexameter couplet with internal Leonine rhymes (for which, see *Annus Mirabilis*, Chapter 3); *prodesse* takes the dative *nulli*; the man in the moon shouldering his burden is a visible warning that theft will bring no benefit to the thief

15.   revoca … ingemisce … erige … suspira – vocatives

16.   clariora … sole – ablative of comparision, 'our bodies will be brighter than the sun'

17.   longe clarior … quam modo – comparison with *quam,* 'the sun will be far brighter than it is now'; *quam* is usually followed by the indicative in Classical usage, but here the subjunctive *sit*

18.   multo … clariora sole – 'much brighter than the sun'; *multo* is the ablative of measure of difference.

3. ON EXPERIMENTAL SCIENCE (ROGER BACON, *c.*1214–1294)

Often hailed as 'the first scientist', Roger Bacon's life and thought have sometimes been obscured by legendary tales of the man known as *Doctor Mirabilis*. Bacon was a Franciscan friar who had studied with the French scholar Peter Peregrinus at Paris (Peregrinus experimented with magnetism and was the first to describe in detail the operation of a compass). Bacon went on to write extensively about almost all branches of contemporary knowledge, radically emphasising the need to use mathematics and to perform experiments. Pope Clement IV commissioned Bacon to write what became an encyclopaedic overview of natural philosophy and its relation to theology – the *Opus Maius* – but when Clement died, Bacon's works and methods attracted accusations of heresy.

In the *Opus Maius* Bacon describes, *inter alia*, gunpowder, microscopes, telescopes, flying machines and ships powered by steam. In his treatment of the science of optics he drew on the works of Islamic scientists who were far more advanced than their European counterparts (as we shall see in Chapter 7, an Arab scholar described the circulation of the blood centuries before William Harvey). In this extract, Bacon outlines his belief in the necessity of making experiments – compare and contrast with the similar opinions expressed by his Elizabethan namesake Francis Bacon in Chapter 7.

> *Duo enim sunt modo cognoscendi, scilicet per argumentum et experimentum. Argumentum concludit et facit nos concedere conclusionem, sed non certificat neque removet dubitationem ut quiescat animus in intuitu veritatis, nisi eam inveniat via experientiae; quia multi habent argumenta ad scibilia, sed quia non habent experientiam, negligunt ea, nec vitant nociva nec persequuntur bona. Si enim aliquis homo qui nunquam vidit ignem probavit per argumenta sufficientia quo ignis comburit et laedit res et destruit, nunquam propter hoc quiesceret animus audientis, nec ignem vitaret antequam poneret manum vel rem combustibilem ad ignem, ut per experientiam probaret quod argumentum edocebat. Sed assumpta experientia combustionis certificatur animus quiescit in fulgore veritatis. Ergo argumentum non sufficit, sed experientia.*

[*Opus Maius*, 6.1]

Notes:

1. argumentum – Bacon means deductive or syllogistic reasoning
2. certificat – a medieval Latin verb (= Italian *certifico*), 'certify the truth of a statement', i.e. a sound deductive argument has nothing to say about whether its conclusion corresponds to something in reality, only that the conclusion necessarily follows from its premises. So, for example, 'All unicorns have horns, Claude is a unicorn, therefore Claude has a horn' is a sound deduction, but no assertion is made about whether unicorns actually exist
3. intuitu veritatis – the mind cannot rest 'in the consideration of truth' by reason alone, it must discover things for itself by means of experience
4. scibilia – neuter plural, 'things knowable', from *scibilis*, a late-Latin adjective

5. quo ignis comburit – 'in what way/how fire burns'
6. vitaret – the person who has heard (*audientis*) the argument would not
    avoid fire until they had practical experience of it
7. assumpta experientia – 'having been acquired by experience'; the fact
    of combustion is verified by experience.

4. ON RAINBOWS (ROGER BACON, *c.*1214–1294)

In this practical demonstration of the kind of experimental science
he advocated, Bacon infers by observation that a rainbow (*iris*) is not
a single, concrete object as some suppose but that there are as many
different rainbows as there are people to observe it. Whenever an
observer moves, the rainbow moves with them; therefore the rainbow
cannot be perceived via incident rays like a solid object but must be
perceived by the reflected rays of the sun.

> *Nam si duo simul stent aspicientes iridem in aquilone, et unus recedat ad occidens, iris*
> *movebitur aequidistanter ei, et si alius vadit ad oriens, iris movetur aequidistanter illi,*
> *vel si stet in loco primo, stabit iris. Manifestum est ergo quod iris numeratur secundum*
> *numerum hominum aspicientium; et ideo impossible est quod duo videant unam*
> *et eandem iridem, quamvis inexpertus hoc non percipiat. Nam umbra cuiuslibet*
> *dividit arcum iridis in duo aequalia, et ideo, cum umbrae sint aequidistantes quoad*
> *sensum, non concurrunt ad medium eiusdem iridis, et ideo cuilibet aspicienti debetur*
> *propria iris. Et hoc patet, quia si in diversas et contrarias partes duae moveantur*
> *iridies, movebuntur secundum motum videntium, et ideo quot sunt videntes, tot sunt*
> *irides. Ex his ergo sequitur quod iris non videtur nisi per radios solis reflexos, quia*
> *si per radios incidentes, tunc esset iris res fixa in uno loco nubis, quae non variaretur*
> *secundum motum aspicientis, neque secundum numerum eorum.*

[*Opus Maius*, 6.7]

Notes:

1. in aquilone … ad occidens … ad oriens – if two people looking north
    perceive a rainbow, and one moves west the other south, the rainbow
    moves equidistantly with them
2. inexpertus – the vulgar opinion
3. umbra cuiuslibet – 'the shadow of each observer'
4. quoad sensum – 'as far as can be perceived'

5. debetur propria iris – 'each individual rainbow is indebted to each onlooker'
6. radios ... reflexos – reflected light, as opposed to *radios incidentes*, 'incident rays', the light from solid objects
7. esset – a hypothetical, 'if it were'.

RECOMMENDED READING

Bacon, R. (ed. Bridges)   *Opus Majus*
    Elibron Classics

A facsimile reprint of John Henry Bridges' 1900 edition.

Clegg, B.   *The First Scientist: A Life of Roger Bacon*
    Carroll & Graf

A modern biography of Bacon's fascinating life and thought.

Map, W. (ed. Wright)   *Gualteri Mapes de Nugis Curialium*
    Kessinger Publications

A facsimile reprint of Thomas Wright's 1850 edition.

Neckam, A. (ed. Wright)   *Alexandri Neckam de Naturis Rerum*
    Kessinger Publications

A facsimile reprint of Thomas Wright's 1863 edition.

CHAPTER 6

RENAISSANCE POETS AND PLAYWRIGHTS

The Renaissance in Britain was stimulated at least in part by close links with continental European writers – Erasmus was a close friend of Thomas More whose *Utopia* (see *Annus Mirabilis*, Chapter 6) was a Latin bestseller in its day. The great Scottish humanist George Buchanan spent much of his time among the intellectual and literary elite of France and Portugal, and Francis Bacon (Chapter 7) received some of his education at the University of Poitiers, where René Descartes also studied.

The break with the recent medieval past can clearly be seen in the new outpouring of Latin poetry, now explicitly modelled on Roman originals. The elegant classicism of the ancients was enthusiastically revived and there were few literary men who did not enjoy writing Latin verse (Shakespeare was unusual in this respect).

But Britain did not just produce Classically inclined poets. Latin drama was also popular – at least at the two English universities – and some 150 plays survive from the period 1550–1650. These plays were given royal approval by both Queen Elizabeth I and her successor James I who attended performances, and they even achieved some fame – as well as notoriety – outside the walls of academe. Thomas Nashe and Christopher Marlowe saw Latin plays at Cambridge, the poet Andrew Marvell acted in one and John Milton was also familiar with them, but had a Puritan's preference for those derived from Scripture rather than profane sources.

1. THE FIRST OF MAY (GEORGE BUCHANAN, 1506–1582)

One of the great figures of Renaissance humanism, George Buchanan, spent many years in continental Europe before returning to his native Scotland as tutor to Mary I (Mary Queen of Scots) and then to her son James VI (later James I of England). As a teacher and scholar he was greatly influential both in Scotland and France, and he was considered the finest Latin writer of his day, an opinion which even such an unlikely champion of Scottish learning as Dr Johnson concurred with, as Boswell relates:

> In a conversation concerning the literary merits of the countries [England and Scotland], in which Buchanan was introduced, a Scotchman, imagining that on this ground he should have an undoubted triumph over him, exclaimed, 'Ah, Dr Johnson, what would you have said of Buchanan, had he been an Englishman?' 'Why, Sir' (said Johnson, after a little pause), 'I should *not* have said of Buchanan, had he been an *Englishman*, what I will now say of him as a *Scotchman* – that he was the only man of genius his country every produced.'
>
> [Boswell, *Life of Johnson*]

Buchanan's Latin works include plays and polemical works (his *De Jure Regni apud Scotos*, 1579, argues that tyrannicide is justified against bad rulers) and a history of Scotland (*Rerum Scoticarum Historia*, 1582). His poetical output was prodigious and eclectic – including paraphrases of the Psalms in Classical metres, scurrilous political and religious satires, and bawdy verses after the manner of Martial and Catullus.

His charming short poem *Calendae Maiae* attracted the praise of Dr Johnson during his Scottish tour. Dr Blair of Edinburgh wrote to Boswell about Johnson's stay in his house:

> Among other subjects, the discourse happening to turn on modern Latin poets, the Dr expressed a very favourable opinion of Buchanan, and instantly repeated, from beginning to end, an ode of his, intitled *Calendae Maiae* (the eleventh in his *Miscellaneorum Liber*), beginning with these words, *Salvete sacris deliciis sacrae*, with which I had formerly been unacquainted; but upon perusing it, the praise which he bestowed upon it, as one of the happiest of Buchanan's poetical compositions, appeared to me very just.
>
> [Boswell, *Journal of a Tour to the Hebrides*, Chapter 12]

The poem modulates from a semi-mythological description of the delights of spring to a meditation on the brevity of life and the need therefore to 'seize the day' inspired in part by Horace and his famous *carpe diem* ode (1.11).

Calendæ Maiae

Salvete, sacris deliciis sacrae
Maiae Calendae, laetitiae et mero,
    ludisque dicatae iocisque
        et teneris Charitum choreis.

Salve, voluptas et nitidum decus
anni recurrens perpetua vice,
    et flos renascentis iuventae,
        in senium properantis aevi.

Cum blanda veris temperies novo
illuxit orbi, primaque saecula
    fulsere flaventi metallo
        sponte sua sine lege iusta,

talis per omnes continuus tenor
annos tepenti rura Favonio
    mulcebat, et nullis feraces
        seminibus recreabat agros.

Talis beatis incubat insulis
felicis aurae perpetuus tepor
    et nesciis campis senectae
        difficilis querulique morbi.

Talis silentum per tacitum nemus
Levi susurrat murmure spiritus
    Lethenque iuxta obliviosam
        funereas agitat cupressos.

Forsan supremis cum Deus ignibus
piabit orbem, laetaque saecula
    mundo reducet, talis aura
        aethereos animos fovebit.

Salve, fugacis gloria saeculi,
salve, secunda digna dies nota
    salve, vetustae vitae imago
        et specimen venientis aevi.

Notes:

1. Metre – Alcaics, see Appendix
2. Maiae Calendae – vocative
3. sacrae – 'sacred/consecrated to' + datives
4. mero – pure (i.e.) undiluted wine
5. dicatae – 'dedicated to' + datives; the 'i' is short, so properly belongs in a light syllable, but like many other Renaissance neo-Latinists Buchanan can be quite flexible with his prosody
6. Charitum – 'of the Graces'; *Charis* was one of the Graces, hence dances of grace and beauty
7. perpetua vice – ablative, 'in unending succession'
8. properantis aevi – take *properantis* with *iuventae* and *aevi* after *in senium*
9. illuxit – 'began to shine on' + dative *novo orbi*
10. fulsere – perfect tense (= *fulserunt*)
11. flaventi metallo – i.e. gold
12. sponte sua ... iusta – 'inherently just'
13. per tacitum – 'silently'.
14. murmure – ablative; the short 'e' scans in a light syllable; most Roman poets avoided placing a short end vowel before a word beginning with two consonants since to do so should (by strict rules of scansion) make that syllable heavy, and for some reason this was felt to be inadmissable; Renaissance versifiers, by contrast, had noted the few exceptions to this rule and then adopted it as fixed practice that a short end vowel before a word beginning with two consonants remained in a light syllable.

2. RICARDUS TERTIUS (THOMAS LEGGE, 1535–1607)

Thomas Legge was Master of Caius College then Vice-Chancellor of Cambridge University. His Latin history play *Ricardus Tertius* was staged at St John's College in 1579. Its novel combination of British history and Classical Latin tragedy after the manner of Seneca made it quite a hit and, despite its great length and large cast, it seems to have been staged on several occasions thereafter. It may have been seen by Christopher Marlowe and Thomas Nashe who thus form a link between it and Shakespeare's later English version – there are sufficient similarities between Legge's treatment and Shakespeare's to suggest that the latter borrowed some elements of his version from the former.

Legge's tragedy is not a single play but a trilogy of plays, each part of which is described as an *Actio*, charting the rise and fall of Richard. In this scene from the third *Actio*, a lady-in-waiting brings news to Queen Elizabeth that her two sons, the princes Richard and Edward, have been murdered in the Tower of London by the King's command.

ANCILLA.

Quando vacabit tempus ullum cladibus
modumque ponet matris attonitae dolor?
Nam triste matri nuncium demens taces?
totas an animus gaudet aerumnas suas
tractare, longos et dolores claudere?
O regio quondam tumens fastu, potens
Regina.

REGINA.

Misera, voce quid media stupes?
exire iussus non reperit viam sonus?
fusisque turpes lachrymis genae madent.

ANCILLA.

Saevit cruento dente frendens aper.

REGINA.

Adhuc
quicquamne restat sceleris?

ANCILLA.

Ah, gnati tui.

REGINA.

Audire cupio miserias statim meas.

ANCILLA.

Heu ambo scelere suffocantur iam principes,
Labefacta mens succumbit: assurge: hei mihi,
rursus cadentem misera spiritum leva.
spirat, revixit, tarda mors miseros fugit.

REGINA.

Regnare nunc sceleste patrue potes, nihil
timebit imbelles ferox pueros furor.
scelesta vibres sceptra: adhuc unum deest
sceleri tuo, iam sanguinem nostrum pete,
tui furoris misera testis haud ero.
Quem defleam infoelix? propinquos? liberos?

anne malis superesse fata quem sinunt
tantis? Ego meos mater occidi, latus
Eduarde quando comite nudavi tuo,
et tunc asylum deseris dulcis puer.
Te, te precor supplex mater genibus minor,
qui vindicas flamas vibras, tonans pater,
et hunc vibrentur tela peiurum tua.
Spolies Olimpum irate fulminibus tuis,
et impium coeli ruina vindicet.

ANCILLA.

Quin placida cogites, animumque mitiga,
mentemque sana turbidam curis leva.

REGINA.

O patrui monstrum nefandum, quale nec
Dirus Procrustes novit, aut Colchos ferox.
O Cardinalis impii fallax fides,
cui filium vesana mandavi meum.
O filii charissimi, o liberi,
quos patrui crudelis ensis eripit,
suo nec unum sufficit sceleri nefas
vestrumque matri funus invident mihi.

[*Actio Tertia, Actus Primus,* III]

Notes:

1. Meter – Iambic senarius, see Appendix
2. vacabit – 'be devoid of', followed by ablative *cladibus*
3. modumque ponet – 'will impose a limit', i.e. 'will her grief come to an end'; the text I have elides all final 'm's, so *modūque* etc., which I have restored for ease of reading
4. demens – the maid thinks herself mad for wishing to be silent about the sad news
5. regio ... fastu – 'once swollen (*tumens*) with royal pride'
6. voce ... media – 'in the midst of speaking'; *iussus ... sonus* – 'the sound which has been ordered out'
7. gnati – *nati*, 'sons'
8. misera ... leva – vocative (*misera*), imperative (*leva*)
9. patrue – vocative, 'o wicked uncle'
10. deest – takes dative *sceleri tuo*

11. malis ... tantis – 'or he whom (*quem*) the fates allowed to have survived (*superesse*) such great evils'

12. nudavi – with ablative *comite tuo*, 'stripped your side (*latus*) of your companion'

13. minor – 'inferior' or 'not equal', i.e. she is unequal to carrying out herself the task she requests

14. flamas – for *flammas*

15. peiurum – 'perjurer' (written in the text as *pjurū*)

16. irate – ablative, 'in your anger' (not the adverb which ends in a long 'e')

17. cogites – subjunctive but equivalent to an imperative; *mitiga ... sana ... leva* are all imperatives

18. Procustes – *Procrustes*, a mythological highwayman who chopped people up or stretched them in order to make them fit onto his bed

19. ferox Colchos – 'the fearsome [woman] of Colchis', i.e. Medea, the Colchian sorceress who killed her own children when their father Jason left her to marry someone else

20. Cardinalis impii – 'of an impious Cardinal'

21. unum ... nefas – 'one unholy deed does not suffice for his wickedness (*sceleri*)', the mother is also denied a funeral.

3. IGNORAMUS (GEORGE RUGGLE, 1575–1621/2)

George Ruggle's comedy *Ignoramus* was first staged at Cambridge in 1614 during a visit to the university by King James I. Written in a macaronic mish-mash of Latin, Anglicised Latin and French, the play satirises pettifogging lawyers and their ridiculous jargon in the person of Ignoramus himself, a pedantic dullard who has travelled to Bordeaux to marry Rosabella. Much complicated toing and froing ensues as Rosabella's true sweetheart Antonius attempts to thwart the avaricious lawyer's nefarious plans. The play was a great success, and continued to be staged well into the eighteenth century (an edition was published as late as 1787). A measure of the play's popularity is that the name of the central character has since passed into common English usage.

In this extract from Act I, Ignoramus is introduced: he has just landed at Bordeaux where he is having a torrid time in the heat and crowds. He talks to his clerks in horrible Anglo-Latin (*Rubba me cum towallio*) peppered with silly legalese. Poor Musaeus (whose name means 'inspired by the Muses', i.e. 'learned') is berated for being the only one to have attended university.

IGNORAMUS, *causidicus*
DULMAN, MUSAEUS, PECUS, *clerici ignorami*

IGNORAMUS: *Phi, phi! Tanta pressa, tantum crowdum ut fui pressus paene ad mortem; habebo actionem de Intrusione contra omnes vos. Aha, Monsieurs, voulez vous intruder par ioyn-tennant? phi phi! valde caleor, cha, cha! precor Deum non meltavi meum pingue; phi, phi! in nomine Dei ubi sunt clerici mei nunc? Dulman, Dulman.*
DULMAN: *Hic Magister Ignoramus, vous avez Dulman.*
IGN: *Meltor, Dulman, meltor. Rubba me cum towallio, rubba. Ubi est Pecus?*
PECUS: *Hic, sir.*
IGN: *Fac ventum, Pecus, ita, sic, sic; ubi est Fled-witt?*
DUL: *Non est inventus.*
IGN: *Ponite nunc chlamydes vestras super me ne capiam frigus. Sic, sic, bien faicte. Inter omnes poenas meas valde laetor et gaudeor nunc quod feci bonum aggreamentum inter Anglos nostros; superinde cras hoisabimus vela et returnabimus iterum erga Londinum; tempus est nam huc venimus Octabis Hilarii et nunc fere est Quindena Paschae.*
DUL: *Iuro, magister, titillasti punctum legis hodie.*
IGN: *Ha ha, puto titillabam.*
PECUS: *Nunquam audivi titillatum melius; quid tu dicis, Musaee?*
MUSAEUS: *Equidem ego parum intellexi.*
IGN: *Tu es galli crista vocatus a Cocks-combe; nunquam faciam te legistam.*
DUL: *Nunquam, nunquam, nam ille fuit universitans.*
IGN: *Sunt magni Idiotae et clerici nihilorum isti universitantes: miror quomodo spendisti tuum tempus inter eos.*
MUS: *Ut plurimum versatus sum in Logica.*
IGN: *Logica? Quae villa, quod burgum est Logica?*
MUS: *Est una artium liberalium.*
IGN: *Liberalium? Sic putabam, in nomine Dei stude artes parcas et lucrosas; non est mundus pro artibus liberalibus iam.*
MUS: *Deditus etiam fui amori Philosophiae.*
IGN: *Amori? quid? es pro baggadgiis et strumpetis? Si custodis malam regulam, non es pro me, rursum reddam te in manus parentum iterum.*
MUS: *Dii faxint.*
IGN: *Quota est clocka nunc?*
DUL: *Est inter octo et nina.*

IGN: *Nina! ite igitur ad mansorium nostrum cum baggis et rotulis, quid id est?*
Videam hoc instrumentum; mane un petit dum calceo spectaculum super nasum.
Oho scio iam: Haec Indentura facta est inter Rogerum Ratledocke de Caxton in
comitatu Brecknock. Oho, Richard Den, John Fen; oho, oho, Proud Buzzarde
plaintiffe adversus Pegoose defendante. Oho, hic est defaulta literae emenda emenda,
nam in nostra lege una comma evertit totum placitum. Ite iam, copiato tu hoc, tu
hoc ingrossa, tu trussato sumptorium pro iurnea.

[Act 1 Scene iii]

Notes:

1. Notes are almost superfluous for much of this passage. Several variant readings are also possible from the many different manuscript sources; this text is based on the facsimile edition in the *Renaissance Latin Drama in England* series (see recommended reading below)
2. chlamydes – cloaks or capes
3. aggreamentum – a legal agreement
4. superinde – adverb, 'on that account'
5. Octabis Hilarii … Quindena Paschae – two terms of Oxford University's academic year, Hilary is the second (post-Christmas), Easter the third
6. galli crista – the crest bone of a cockerel
7. legistam – Medieval Latin for a lawyer (*legista* also Italian, Spanish, Portuguese)
8. ut plurimum – 'for the most part'
9. baggadgiis – 'baggage'
10. faxint – alternative form of *fecerint*
11. rotulis – literally, 'little wheels' but presumably here = rolls or scrolls, the lawyer's legal papers
12. indentura – a legal term for a deed between two parties
13. copiato … ingrossa … trussato – imperatives of Medieval Latin *copiare*, 'to copy' (Italian), *ingrossare*, 'to make a fair copy' and and *trussare*, 'to pack'
14. sumptorium – or *sumptorum*, 'our possessions' (from *sumere*, 'to take possession of'); *iurnea* – 'journey'.

4. IN BARVITIUS' GARDEN (ELIZABETH JANE WESTON, 1581–1612)

Although born in England, Elizabeth Weston spent much of her life in continental Europe, especially in Prague, and it was there that she achieved recognition for her Latin poetry. Weston's father had died when she was still an infant and her mother then married Edward Kelley, an associate of Dr John Dee, Elizabeth I's court astrologer. When Dee and Kelley travelled to the court of the Holy Roman Emperor King Rudolf II, Elizabeth and her siblings went with them. But Dee returned to England and Kelley died in 1597, leaving his widow and children destitute. Much of Elizabeth's poetry from this period, collected in her first book *Poemata* (1602), was addressed in flattering terms to potential benefactors at court.

Elizabeth married in 1603 and thus restored her family's fortunes, but she continued to write Latin verse for which she was highly praised. Another volume was published in 1609 under the title *Parthenicon*, the 'Maidenly Writings' of the *Virginis nobilissimae, poetriae florentissimae, linguarum plurimarum peritissimae.*

One of her patrons at Rudolf's court was Johann Barvitius, the emperor's secretary whose elegant gardens Weston extols as a reflection of their owner's cultivated mind.

In Hortos Eiusdem

Hortus odoratis hic est cultissimus herbis,
    Barviti assidua cultus, et altus ope.
Hic, quoties lassum te Caesaris aula remittit,
    A curis relevas pectora fessa tuis.
Hic locus est fidis etiam concessus amicis;
    Hic datur aspectu colloquioque frui.
Hic audire preces viduarum, et vota clientum
    Suscipere, innata pro bonitate, soles.
Sic Domino servit decoratus floribus hortus:
    Atque horti Dominus gaudet honore sui.
Quid precer huic igitur? ne vel Zephyritida Cauri
    Aut Euri rabies impetuosa fuget.
Sed vireat variis ita fructibus, atque quotannis
    Suppeditet Domino munera grata suo.
Quidve precer Domino? ne laedat livor in aula,
    Virtuti semper qui comes esse solet.

[*Parthenicon, Liber* I]

Notes:

1. Metre – elegiac couplets, see Appendix
2. eiusdem – in Weston's book this follows several other poems also addressed to Barvitius
3. cultissimus … cultus – a pun: the first refers to the garden, the second (genitive) to Barvitius himself, a man of culture
4. assidua … ope – ablative, 'by constant effort'
5. altus – also referring to the *hortus*, perfect participle of *alo*, 'nurtured'
6. datur – impersonal passive: literally, 'it is granted (to you)'
7. frui – intransitive followed by ablatives *aspectu colloquioque*
8. suscipere – to take up or discharge the wishes (*vota*) of his clients
9. precer huic – *precor* takes the dative in the sense of 'pray for, ask for', *huic* here refers to the garden; the construction is repeated in the penultimate line with *Domino*
10. Zephyritida – the gentle western breezes, accusative plural after *ne … fuget*: this is a classical allusion borrowed from Catullus, who in Poem 66 puns on the temple of Aphrodite Zephyritis (at Zephyrium near Alexandria), which means 'having power over Zephyrium' but also 'having power over Zephyrus', i.e. the west wind; Weston asks that the north and east winds do not drive away the gentler west.

5. CRUEL FATE (GEORGE HERBERT, 1593–1633)

As a clever young Cambridge graduate George Herbert was much in favour at the court of King James I. But after the King's death in 1625, Herbert forsook the pleasures of courtly life for retirement as a country parson, first at Leighton Bromswold in Cambridgeshire then at Bemerton, Wiltshire. But there the consumption which had made his constitution fragile for many years finally overtook him; as his health rapidly declined he turned increasingly to spiritual matters in both his Latin and English poetry.

Herbert's book of English poetry, *The Temple of Sacred Poems and Private Ejaculations*, was not published until the year of his death. His other works were collected and published posthumously. Herbert's father had died when he was still an infant, so he formed a very close bond with his mother. Her death, shortly after he had taken religious orders, caused an outpouring of grief which he expressed in a series of heartfelt Latin poems collectively entitled *Parentalia*. In this short ode, Herbert rails against the cruel fate (*malignum sidus*) that has taken his mother from him and shaken his determination to pursue the 'pious path' (*piam semitam*):

> Parvam piamque dum lubenter semitam
>   Grandi reaeque praefero,
> Carpsit malignum sidus hanc modestiam
>   Vinumque felle miscuit.
> Hinc fremere totus et minari gestio
>   Ipsis severus orbibus;
> Tandem prehensa comiter lacernula
>   Susurrat aure quispiam,
> Haec fuerat olim potio Domini tui.
>   Gusto proboque dolium.

[*Parentalia* VIII]

Notes:

1. Metre – iambic, see Appendix; Herbert's metrical scheme is modelled on Horace's epode 2.1, *Beatus ille procul negotiis / ut prisca gens mortalium*
2. praefero – here followed by accusative (*parvam piamque semitam*) then dative of that to which it is preferred (*grandi reaeque*, understand *semitae*)
3. carpsit – 'snatched away' or 'eroded'; *malignum sidus* – the evil fate which took his mother from him
4. felle – 'bitter bile', i.e. the bitterness of grief
5. fremere – not the infinitive (short middle 'e' hence a light syllable) but the contracted form of *fremuerunt*, which has a long middle 'e', *fremēre*; subject is *totus*: 'every part of me cried out'
6. minari – after *gestio*, 'I long to threaten', followed by dative *ipsis orbibus; severus* – adverbial, 'severely'
7. prehensa ... lacernula – ablative absolute (the long 'a' of *prehens* makes the third foot a trochee); *lacernula* is the diminutive of *lacerna*, 'a cloak' – a friend (*quispiam*) has attracted his attention by taking hold of his cloak in a friendly manner (*comiter*)
8. dolium – an earthenware vessel for storing liquids, so by metonymy the drink itself.

RECOMMENDED READING:

Binns, J.W. (ed.)   *The Latin Poetry of English Poets*
Routledge & Kegan Paul

Includes an essay on George Herbert among others.

Ford, P.J.   *George Buchanan: Prince of Poets*
Aberdeen University Press

A study of Buchanan's poetry, with a complete edition of the
Miscellaneorum Liber (edited by W.S. Watt)

Stevenson, J.   *Women Latin Poets*
Oxford University Press

Includes a discussion of Elizabeth Weston's poetry.

Legge and Ruggle   *Renaissance Latin Drama in England*
George Olms

Both plays are available in this series of facsimile editions of handwritten
manuscripts. For ease of reading, Dana F. Sutton's online texts are
preferable:
Ricardus Tertius   http://www.philological.bham.ac.uk/rich/
Ignoramus   http://www.philological.bham.ac.uk/ruggle/

For those with deep pockets, John Sidney Hawkins' 1787 edition of
Ignoramus was reprinted in 2006 by the Lawbook Exchange (ISBN
1584776757).

Weston (ed. Cheney) *Poemata* and *Parthenicon*
Ashgate

A scholarly edition of Weston's poetry, together with the works of
another female Latin poet, Bathusa Reginald (Makin).

CHAPTER 7

THE AGE OF ENLIGHTENMENT

As the universal language of scholarship both before and after the Renaissance, Latin was the language in which many of the great scientific advances of the modern age were expressed – from Copernicus and Galileo (see *Annus Mirabilis*, Chapter 6) to the classifying of *flora* and *fauna* by Linnaeus (*Annus Horribilis*, Chapter 6) and many others besides. In Britain, Latin scientific writing took on a distinctively empirical tone after Bacon's advocacy of inductive method encouraged a new spirit of practical enquiry. Bacon's spirit lives on in Harvey's rigorous investigations concerning the circulation of the blood. But after the publication of Newton's seminal *Principia* something other than Latin began to take over as the new universal language of science – Newton wrote in Latin because it remained an important way of communicating with the international community of scholars, but his Latin was subordinate to his mathematics. Latin's value as a scientific *lingua franca* was about to be replaced: after Newton, scientific arguments would increasingly be expressed in terms of equations.

1. ON THE BENEFITS OF MUSIC (JOHN CASE, 1539/46–1600)

John Case was an Oxford scholar who wrote and lectured principally on the logic and philosophy of Aristotle. But during his lifetime the Puritans had become greatly exercised about the immorality of the theatrical arts, including music. Case's *Apologia Musices Tam Vocalis Quam Instrumentalis et Mixtae*, 'An apology for music both vocal as well as instrumental and mixed' (1588) is a riposte to the Puritans, in which the author sets out to show that music is morally improving and deserves its place both in social settings and especially in church.

Case begins by noting that music has three uses: religious, ethical and political. Having already spoken of its divine use, he now turns to the moral use of music – Case's citing of Aristotle and his use of arguments concerned with morality put him firmly in the pre-Baconian camp.

Sed ut in pauca rem totam conferam, usus musices triplex est, divinus qui contemplationem, ethicus qui institutionem vitae, politicus qui conservationem reipublicae ac civitatis spectat. De theorico et divino satis diximus, de ethico et civili nunc pauca dicemus. Ethicus seu moralis usus musices (ut distinguendo procedam) in duobus precipue cernitur, nempe in sedandis malis affectibus et in bonis moribus comparandis: hinc est quod Aristoteles aliique Philosophi persuaserint pueros et adolescentes ad studium et praxim musices cogendos, cuius rei causae tres sunt, quia in ea est expressa imago et dulcedo virtutis, utilis excercitatio vocis, moderatio affectus. Imago virtutis: est enim musica ipsa virtus; virtutis dulcedo, est enim musica ipsa concentus; exercitatio vocis, est enim in praxi musices salutaris agitatio pulmonis, quae generosum spiritum et calorem in praecordiis gignit, crassos humores (quibus abundat aetas puerilis) digerit, omnesque vapores et nubes a capite fluentes aut fluxas pellit; postremo moderatio affectus in ea inest, quia ut antea docuimus, per aerem auremque in ipsam mentem agit, eamque mirabiliter sub suo nutu et imperio tenet.

[*Apologia Musices Tam Vocalis Quam Instrumentalis et Mixtae,* 7.2]

Notes:

1. sed ... conferam – 'but to summarise the whole matter in a few [words]'
2. qui ... spectat – 'which is concerned with'
3. distinguendo – 'to proceed by making a distinction'
4. in sedandis ... in comparandis – 'in restraining evil emotions and in acquiring good morals'
5. persuaserint – 'recommended'; perfect subjunctive in an indirect question (*quod*, 'why')
6. praxim – accusative of *praxis*, a Greek loan-word, 'practice'
7. cogendos – gerundive of obligation with *pueros*, 'ought to be compelled'
8. affectus – genitive singular
9. concentus – 'harmony'
10. generosum ... in praecordiis – 'a noble respiration and heat in the vitals'
11. fluentes aut fluxas – 'flowing or which have flowed from the head (*a capite*)'
12. in ea inest – 'enters into those things', i.e. the moderation of emotion happens because ...
13. sub suo nutu et imperio – music 'holds the mind under its own approbation and power'.

2. AGAINST SUPERSTITION (FRANCIS BACON, 1561–1626)

Francis Bacon represents a significant break with the past, and especially with the scholastic thinking of the medieval period when natural philosophers relied upon the logic of Aristotle and the authority of Scripture in order to make conclusions about the world around them. For Bacon, by contrast, the business of doing science was an entirely practical matter, consisting not of abstract reasoning or appealing to dogma, but of observation, experiment and the forming of rational conclusions based on observed empirical phenomena. Bacon expounded his version of this inductive method in the *Novum Organum* (1620) so-called because it contained a new alternative to Aristotle's deductive (syllogistic) method as set forth in his works on logic, collectively known as the *Organon*. In his 1837 essay on Bacon, Macaulay mockingly contrasted the approach of ancient philosophers and their idealistic schemes with the practical empiricism of Bacon's new method.

> We have sometimes thought that an amusing fiction might be written, in which a disciple of Epictetus and a disciple of Bacon should be introduced as fellow-travellers. They come to a village where the smallpox has just begun to rage, and find houses shut up, intercourse suspended, the sick abandoned, mothers weeping in terror over their children. The Stoic assures the dismayed population that there is nothing bad in the smallpox, and that to a wise man disease, deformity, death, the loss of friends, are not evils. The Baconian takes out a lancet and begins to vaccinate.
>
> [Macaulay, *Francis Bacon*, 1837]

The *Novum Organum* begins with a series of aphorisms in which Bacon uses wit and the ability to tell a good story as much as argument to demolish what he calls the worshipping of *idola*. In this aphorism, Bacon attacks one of the 'Idols of the Theatre', that is those dogmatic beliefs arising from superstition or other false systems which represent the world in as unreal and scenic a manner as a theatre. Next time you read your horoscope, spare a thought for Bacon.

Intellectus humanus in iis quae semel placuerunt (aut quia recepta sunt et credita, aut
quia delectant), alia etiam omnia trahit ad suffragationem et consensum cum illis: et
licet maior sit instantiarum vis et copia, quae occurrunt in contrarium, tamen eas aut
non observat, aut contemnit, aut distinguendo summovet et reiicit, non sine magno
et pernicioso praeiudicio, quo prioribus illis syllepsibus authoritas maneat inviolata.
Itaque recte respondit ille, qui, cum suspensa tabula in templo ei monstraretur eorum
qui vota solverant, quod naufragii periculo elapsi sint, atque interrogando premeretur,
anne tum quidem Deorum numen agnosceret, quaesivit denuo, At ubi sunt illi depicti
qui post vota nuncupata perierint? Eadem ratio est fere omnis superstitionis, ut in
astrologicis, in somniis, ominibus, nemesibus, et huiusmodi in quibus homines delectati
huiusmodi vanitatibus advertunt eventus, ubi emplentur; ast ubi fallunt, licet multo
frequentius, tamen negligunt et praetereunt.

[*Novum Organum* 1.46]

Notes:

1. in iis quae – 'in support of those things which'; *semel placuerunt* – 'were once generally accepted', i.e. the superstitions whose validity Bacon is attacking

2. ad suffragationem – 'to support and be in agreement with them'

3. licet – 'although'; *instantiarum* – 'applications, instances'

4. distinguendo – 'by drawing a distinction'

5. quo … maneat – a result clause with *quo* because it contains a comparative (*prior*)

6. syllepsibus – strictly speaking a *syllepsis* is a grammatical sleight of hand in which one word is used to govern two or more others though not agreeing in gender, number or case with them; translate as 'erroneous conclusions'

7. ille – an unnamed man who, when shown a painting in a temple of those who had escaped shipwreck (*naufragium*) after making vows to the gods, replied 'But where are the pictures of those who had made those vows and then died?'

8. interrogando premeretur – 'he was being pressed by being asked'

'Bacon's greatest performance is the first book of the *Novum Organum*. All the peculiarities of his extraordinary mind are found there in the highest perfection. Many of the aphorisms, but particularly those in which he gives examples of the influence of the idola, show a nicety of observation that has never been surpassed. Every part of the book blazes with wit, but with wit which is so employed only to illustrate and decorate truth.' Macaulay, *Francis Bacon*, 1837.

9. denuo – 'in turn'
10. nemesibus – 'divine retributions', from *Nemesis*, the goddess of retribution
11. ubi emplentur – men only notice the instances in which the dreams, omens, predictions and so forth are fulfilled; they neglect those far more frequent instances in which they are not.

3. ANTS, SPIDERS AND BEES (FRANCIS BACON, 1561–1626)

Bacon did not argue that empirical observation was sufficient in itself – in this aphorism he compares his method to that of the bee who not only gathers but also transforms what it has gathered into something new. The rationalists who rely on deductive knowledge, like spiders can only spin with what they already have; empiricists like ants collect but do not apply their intellect – the bee's mixture of the two methods, experiment and reason, is the right one.

> *Qui tractaverunt scientias aut empirici aut dogmatici fuerunt. Empirici, formicae more, congerunt tantum, et utuntur: rationales, aranearum more, telas ex se conficiunt: apis vero ratio media est, quae materiam ex floribus horti et agri elicit; sed tamen eam propria facultate vertit et digerit. Neque absimile philosophiae verum opificium est; quod nec mentis viribus tantum aut praecipue nititur, neque ex historia naturali et mechanicis experimentis praebitam materiam, in memoria integram, sed in intellectu mutatam et subactam, reponit. Itaque ex harum facultatum (experimentalis scilicet et rationalis) arctiore et sanctiore foedere (quod adhuc factum non est) bene sperandum est.*

[*Novum Organum*, 1.95]

Notes:

1. qui tractaverunt – 'those who have had dealings with'
2. propria facultate – 'with its own particular skill'
3. absimile – 'dissimilar'
4. praebitam materiam – 'material gathered from natural history and mechanical experiments'
5. arctiore et sanctiore foedere – 'from a closer and purer federation'
6. bene sperandum est – gerundive of obligation: 'we ought to have high hopes'.

4. ON THE CIRCULATION OF THE BLOOD (WILLIAM HARVEY, 1578–1657)

Ever since the work of the great Greco-Roman physician Galen (second century AD), a distinction had been made between venous and arterial blood – Galen wrote that the former originated in the liver, the latter in the heart, and that after it had been distributed around the body blood was consumed in the tissues and organs. Galen's authority on this matter (as in many others – for example, the practice of bloodletting) was accepted for centuries. But as early as the thirteenth century a Syrian physician and writer, Ibn Al-Nafis, had discovered the secret of pulmonary circulation. Though his work was not available in Europe, by the sixteenth century some European anatomists were also beginning to describe circulatory systems.

But it was left to William Harvey not only to provide a complete and correct description of both pulmonary circulation (i.e. the carrying of deoxygenated blood from the heart to the lungs and the return of oxygenated blood to the heart) as well as systemic circulation (the carrying of oxygenated blood from the heart to the tissues and the return of deoxygenated blood to the heart) but also to provide copious – indeed irrefutable – evidence drawn from painstaking experiment, dissection and observation. In a brilliant display of the effectiveness of the Baconian method, Harvey was the first to recognise that the heart actually pumped – as opposed to sucked – blood, and he was the first to calculate exactly how much blood is pumped every time the heart beats; he was also the first correctly to observe and describe the function of valves in veins.

Harvey published his findings in *Exercitatio Anatomica De Motu Cordis et Sanguinis in Animalibus*, 'An anatomical exercise concerning the motion of the heart and blood in living organisms', in 1628. In the following extract, he begins by expressing concern that the authority of ancient authors is so fixed that few will take what he has to say seriously. But his love of truth compels him to reveal the facts he has discovered, namely that so great a quantity of blood is pumped by the heart that this blood cannot possibly be created by the organs and ingested by the tissues, instead it must circulate around the body through the arteries and return via the veins to be pumped again.

De copia sanguinis transeuntis per cor e venis in arterias, et de circulari motu sanguinis.

Huc usque de transfusione sanguinis e venis in arterias, et de viis, per quas pertranseat, et quomodo ex pulsu cordis, transmittat et dispenset, de quibus forsan sunt aliqui, qui, antea aut Galeni authoritate aut Columbi aliorumve rationibus adductis, assenturi se dicant mihi; nunc vero, de copia et proventu istius pertranseuntis sanguinis, quae restant (licet valde digna consideratu) cum dixero, adeo nova sunt et inaudita, ut non solum ex invidia quorundam, metuam malum mihi, sed verear ne habeam inimicos omnes homines, tantum consuetudo aut semel imbibita doctrina, altisque defixa radicibus, quasi altera natura, apud omnes valet, et antiquitatis veneranda suspicio cogit. Utcumque iam iacta est alea, spes mea in amore veritatis et doctorum animorum candore: sane cum copia quanta fuerat tam ex vivorum, experimenti causa, dissectione et arteriarum apertione, disquisitione multimoda; tum ex ventriculorum cordis et vasorum ingredientium et egredientium Symmetria et magnitudine (cum natura nihil facies frustra, tantam magnitudinem, proportionabiliter his vasibus frustra non tribuerit) tum ex concinno et diligenti valvularum et fibrarum artificio, reliquaque cordis fabrica, tum ex aliis multis saepius mecum et serio considerassem et animo diutius evoluissem: quanta scilicet esset copia transmissi sanguinis, quam brevi tempore ea transmissio fieret, nec suppeditare ingesti alimenti succum potuisse animadverterim, quin venas inanitas, omnino exhaustas et arterias ex altera parte, nimia sanguinis intrusione, disruptas, haberemus, nisi sanguis aliquo ex arteriis denuo in venas remearet et ad cordis dextrum ventriculum regrederetur.

Coepi egomet mecum cogitare, an motionem quandam quasi in circulo haberet, quam postea veram esse reperi et sanguinem e corde per arterias in habitum corporis et omnes partes protudi et impelli, a sinistri cordis ventriculi pulsu, quemadmodum in pulmones per venam arteriosam a dextris; et rursus per venas in venam cavam et usque ad auriculam dextram remeari, quemadmodum ex pulmonibus per arteriam dictam venosam, ad sinistrum ventriculum ut ante dictum est. Quem motum circularem eo pacto nominare liceat.

[*Exercitatio Anatomica De Motu Cordis et Sanguinis in Animalibus*, 8]

Notes:

1. huc usque – 'thus far', understand a verb such as *dixi*
2. pertranseat ... transmittat et dispenset – all subjunctives in subordinate clauses
3. rationibus adductis – ablative absolute, 'with their reasonings having been influenced'; perhaps there are those who though under the influence of earlier authorities might still give their assent (*assenturi*

se dicant) to Harvey's findings so far; Realdo Colombo or Renaldus
Columbus was a sixteenth-century Italian anatomist who made
important discoveries about pulmonary circulation in his book *De Re
Anatomica* (1559)

4. copia et proventu – 'the quantity and progress'

5. quae restant – 'what remains to be said'; *licet* – 'although'

6. ut non solum – not only does he fear harm from those who are jealous,
    but that he might make everyone his enemy

7. altera natura – to such an extent (*tantum*) does custom or learning
    become fixed and plant deep roots that it becomes second nature and
    prevails with all (*apud omnes valet*)

8. antiquitatis veneranda suspicio cogit – 'the slightest hint (*suspicio*) of
    antiquity compels veneration', i.e. anything that has ancient authority
    is not lightly challenged

9. alea iacta est – Caesar's famous saying upon crossing the Rubicon, 'the
    die is cast'

10. candore – 'whiteness' hence 'purity' hence 'disposition to think well'
    (English 'candour'); *doctorum animorum* – 'of learned minds'

11. cum copia quanta fuerat tam – the *cum* belongs to the verb (greatly
    delayed) *considerassem*, 'after I had often and honestly (*saepius mecum et
    serio*) remarked to myself'

12. ex vivorum … dissectione – this is the only way Harvey could see the
    living heart in action; *experimenti causa* – 'for the sake of proof'

13. disquisitione multimoda – 'in a many-fold inquiry'; take after *cum
    considerassem*

14. cum natura … non tribuerit – 'since no appearance (*facies*) is to no
    purpose (*frustra*), nature would not have allotted (*non tribuerit*) to these
    vessels (*his vasibus*) in vain (*frustra*) such a size in proportion'

15. concinno et diligenti … artificio – 'from the arrangement and careful
    contrivance'; *tum … tum* – 'both … and'

16. evolvissem – also dependent on the much earlier *cum*: 'and after I had
    for a long time turned over in my mind'

17. nec suppeditare ingesti alimenti – 'I had noticed (*animadverterim*) that the
    fluid of ingested food was not able to supply its place'; i.e. the amount
    of blood flowing through the heart could not possibly be created from
    ingested fluid; *quin* – 'but that', if this were the case the veins would be
    empty and the arteries burst from excess

18. denuo … remearet – 'it could in some way (*aliquo*) make its way refreshed'

19. veram esse – accusative + infinitive after *reperi*, followed by the same
     construction, *sanguinem … protudi et impelli … remeari*, 'that the blood
     was thrust forward and driven … that it makes its way'

20. venam arteriosam – the arterial vein or pulmonary artery proceeds
     from the heart like an artery but carries deoxygenated blood to the
     lungs (*in pulmones*)

21. eo pacto – 'by that means'; *liceat nominare* – 'may be called'.

5. THE THREE LAWS OF MOTION (ISAAC NEWTON, 1643–1727)

Perhaps the single most important text in the history of science was
written in Latin. Newton's *Principia Mathematica* (1687) expounds, as
the full title says, the 'Mathematical Principles of Natural Philosophy',
including his theory of universal gravitation – Newton borrowed
the Latin word *gravitas* to describe the force that held the planets in
their orbits. The *Principia* is divided into three books, the first two of
which – subtitled *De motu corporum* – contain mathematical definitions
and deductions about the motions of bodies in general. In the third
book – *De mundi systemate* – Newton applies these mathematical
deductions to the motions of planets and other celestial bodies such
as comets. Herein lies his revolutionary breakthrough: he realised that
considerations about how specific bodies interact with each other (e.g.
apples falling from trees onto a person's head) are applicable universally
– and hence could be used to explain the hitherto mysterious nature
of the orbits of the planetary bodies around the sun which, he could
then deduce, are governed by the inverse square law of gravitation (i.e.
the force of gravity is inversely related to the square of the distance
between two bodies).

The *Principia* starts with a series of mathematical principles
(*definitiones*), which are followed by three 'axioms or Laws of Motion'.
Each begins with a plain statement of the axiom, followed by a second
paragraph in which examples of the law in action are given.

Axiomata, sive Leges Motus

*Lex I: Corpus omne perseverare in statu suo quiescendi vel movendi uniformiter in
directum, nisi quatenus a viribus impressis cogitur statum illum mutare.*

Proiectilia perseverant in motibus suis, nisi quatenus a resistentia aeris retarduntur, et vi gravitatis impelluntur deorsum. Trochus, cuius partes cohaerendo perpetuo retrahunt sese a motibus rectilineis, non cessat rotari, nisi quatenus ab aere retardatur. Maiora autem Planetarum et Cometarum corpora motus suos et progressivos et circulares in spatiis minus resistentibus factos conservant diutius.

Notes:

1. corpus … perseverare – accusative + infinitive
2. quiescendi vel movendi – gerunds
3. nisi quatenus – 'except so far as'
4. proiectilia – 'projectiles'; this seems to be a Newtonian coinage, a diminutive (neuter) of *proiectum* from *proicio*, 'throw out'
5. trochus – a hoop or perhaps a spinning top; any object that is spinning will keep spinning except insofar as it is retarded by the air
6. cohaerendo perpetuo – 'by a perpetual holding together', i.e. the cohesion of an object prevents its individual elements flying off in a straight line (*motibus rectilineis*)
7. maiora … corpora – they behave the same way as the *trochus*, only spin longer because offered less resistance in space.

Lex II: Mutationem motus proportionalem esse vi motrici impressae, et fieri secundum lineam rectam qua vis illa imprimitur.

Si vis aliqua motum quemvis generet; dupla duplum, tripla triplum generabit, sive simul et semel, sive gradatim et successive impressa fuerit. Et hic motus (quoniam in eandem semper plagam cum vi generatrice determinatur) si corpus antea movebatur, motui eius vel conspiranti additur, vel contrario subducitur, vel obliquo oblique adiicitur, et cum eo secundum utriusque determinationem componitur.

Notes:

1. mutationem … proportionalem esse – accusative + infinitive
2. motus – genitive
3. motrici – dative of *motrix*, feminine form of *motor*, agreeing with *vi*, 'motive force applied (*impressae*)'
4. fieri – also accusative + infinitive, 'and that it (the *mutationem*) happens …'
5. dupla duplum, tripla triplum – the change in motion is directly proportional to the amount of force applied: twice the force, twice the change and so forth
6. eandem … plagam – 'the same region'; *generatrice* – feminine (*generatrix*) agreeing with *vi*, 'the generating force'

7. motui eius … conspiranti – 'to its combined motion'
8. obliquo oblique adiicitur – 'mixed obliquely with the oblique motion'
9. secundum determinationem – 'according to the determination of each'; *determinatio* is a technical term meaning the directionality of a body in motion.

Lex III: Actioni contrariam semper et aequalem esse reactionem: sive corporum duorum actiones in se mutuo semper esse aequales et in partes contrarias dirigi.

Quicquid premit vel trahit alterum, tantundem ab eo premitur vel trahitur. Si quis lapidem digito premit, premitur et huius digitus a lapide. Si equus lapidem funi alligatum trahit, retrahetur etiam et equus (ut ita dicam) aequaliter in lapidem: nam funis utrinque distentus eodem relaxandi se conatu urgebit equum versus lapidem, ac lapidem versus equum; tantumque impediet progressum unius quantum promovet progressum alterius. Si corpus aliquod in corpus aliud impingens, motum eius vi sua quomodocunque mutaverit, idem quoque vicissim in motu proprio eandem mutationem in partem contrariam vi alterius (ob aequalitatem pressionis mutuae) subibit. His actionibus aequales fiunt mutationes, non velocitatum, sed motuum; scilicet in corporibus non aliunde impeditis. Mutationes enim velocitatum, in contrarias itidem partes factae, quia motus aequaliter mutantur, sunt corporibus reciproce proportionales.

[*Philosophiae Naturalis Principia Mathematica*, Book I *Axiomata*]

Notes:

1. contrariam … et aequalem esse reactionem – accusative + infinitive; *actioni* – dative
2. in se mutuo – 'jointly together'
3. dirigi – 'is directed towards', passive infinitive
4. tantundem – 'just as much'; examples follow – if someone (*si quis*) presses a stone with their finger, the finger is equally pressed, if a horse drags a stone bound with a rope (*funi alligatum*), the horse is dragged equally
5. ut ita dicam – 'so to speak'
6. utrinque distentus – 'stretched in both directions'
7. eodem relaxandi se conatu – the rope tries to slacken itself and in doing so exerts a force equally in both directions
8. quomodocunque – 'in whatever way'
9. in partem contrariam – the body exhibits a change in its motion on the opposite side to that of the force acting on it
10. pressionis mutuae – 'of mutual pressure'

11. non velocitatum, sed motuum – the changes are not of velocity but of
     motion

12. itidem – 'in the same way'.

RECOMMENDED READING

Modern Latin editions:

Bacon   *Novum Organum and Associated Texts* (Vol. XI of The
              Oxford Francis Bacon)
              Clarendon Press

Newton   *Philosophiae Naturalis Principia Mathematica*
              Elibron Classics (facsimile reprint of a 1739 edition)

CHAPTER 8

AUGUSTAN POETS

Classical learning flourished in Britain in the eighteenth century, a period celebrated as a new Augustan Age. Latin verse composition was a staple of every boy's education at the great public schools, and the ability to compose elegant distychs or verse epistles in Latin was the mark of a cultured gentleman. Horace was the Roman poet whose influence proved to be the most telling – his elegantly lyrical verses often addressed to members of his own close circle of friends found favour in an age that prided itself on its decorum and sensibility. Writers up to and including Dr Johnson found the Horatian ode the most congenial verse form in which to express refined sentiments (for Johnson's poetry see *Annus Mirabilis*, Chapter 7). Tastes change, however, and when Walter Savage Landor published his first Latin poetry in 1795, he chose the more robust Ovid and Catullus as his models.

By the nineteenth century the impetus both for composing and reading new Latin verse was waning fast. Such an ardent amateur classicist as Macaulay, who eagerly devoured every Latin and Greek author, does not seem to have been acquainted with Landor's Latin. The two met on a handful of occasions, but they do not seem to have had much in common – Landor the high-minded Latinist, Macaulay the populist who, though steeped in the Classics, chose to write his *Lays of Ancient Rome* (as every schoolboy once knew) in English.

1. FABULA CANIS ET UMBRAE (JONATHAN SWIFT, 1667–1745)

Unlike the other writers featured in this chapter, the author of *Gulliver's Travels* and *A Modest Proposal* did not dedicate his life to Latin verse. He wrote far less in Latin than his friend and contemporary Joseph Addison (see *Annus Mirabilis*, Chapter 7) though like any educated man of his age he was perfectly capable of doing so when the mood took him – whether in humorous verse epistles to his friend Joseph Sheridan, or in a description of Carbery Rocks (*Carberiae Rupes*). He even wrote his own Latin epitaph (see *Annus Horribilis*, Chapter 15).

In this miniature, Swift casts one of Aesop's fables into Latin hexameters. Carrying food in its mouth, a foolish dog sees an even tastier morsel reflected in the water, but is frustrated when it attempts to snatch what it thought was a better meal.

> *Ore cibum portans catulus dum spectat in undis,*
> *Apparet liquido praedae melioris imago:*
> *Dum speciosa diu damna admiratur, et alte*
> *Ad latices inhiat, cadit imo vortice praeceps*
> *Ore cibus, nec non simulacrum corripit una.*
> *Occupat ille avidus deceptis faucibus umbram;*
> *Illudit species, ac dentibus aera mordet.*

Notes:

1. Metre – hexameters, see Appendix
2. imago – nominative, the image of a better morsel (*praedae melioris*)
3. speciosa … damna – 'the unobtainable spectacle'; *admiratur* is deponent
4. ad latices – 'over the stream'; *latex* is running water or other liquid
5. cadit – the subject is *cibus* on the next line; *imo vortice* – 'to the depths of the swirling water'
6. nec non – 'and also'; *una* – adverb, 'at the same time the likeness (*simulacrum*) snatches it away (*corripuit*)'
7. avidus – the puppy, translate as an adverb, 'greedily'; *deceptis faucibus* – 'with deluded jaws'
8. illudit – the image (*species*) deceives him.

2. CANIS ET ECHO (VINCENT BOURNE, 1694–1747)

Little is known of the life of Vincent Bourne, perhaps the most accessible of all the Anglo-Latin poets. He was educated at Westminster School, England's nursery for eighteenth-century Latinists, and after Cambridge returned there to teach a new generation, including the poet William Cowper who always held his former teacher in great affection and said of him,

I love the memory of Vinny Bourne. I think him a better Latin poet than Tibullus, Propertius, Ausonius, or any of the writers in his way, except Ovid, and not at all inferior to him.

AUGUSTAN POETS

91

Cowper's estimate seemed, for a time at least, to be shared by many others – Bourne's *Poematia* of 1734 had appeared in nine separate editions by 1840. Less overtly indebted to Horace than many of his contemporaries, Bourne's poetry is, as Estelle Haan puts it, 'a fusion of the classical and the romantic'. His wry observations on the vanities of life are given additional piquancy by many

'Do we believe that Erasmus and Fracastorius wrote Latin as well as Dr Robertson and Sir Walter Scott wrote English? ... But does it follow, because we think thus, that we can find nothing to admire in the noble alcaics of Gray, or in the playful elegiacs of Vincent Bourne? Surely not.' Macaulay, *Joseph Addison*, 1843.

allusions to the shortness of that life. As he confessed to a friend,

> It must be the frequent perusal of gravestones and monuments, and the many walks I have taken in a churchyard, that have given me so great a distaste for life; the usual sight of mortality, corruption, and nakedness, must inevitably lead one to a serious reflection on the vanity of all worldly greatness.

In this clever elegy, Bourne adapts and expands upon the Aesop fable Latinised by Swift (above). Here the silly dog snarling at the moon's reflection in the Thames is heard by the nymph Echo, who decides to tease it. Bourne wittily expresses Echo's game in a series of verbal echoes before giving us the moral in the final line: all anger is futile and is reflected back upon itself.

> *Puris in coelo radiis argentea Luna*
> *In Tamisis tremula luce refulsit aquis.*
> *Improbus hic vidit catulus, ringensque malignum*
> *Solvit in indignos ora proterva modos:*
> *Lunamque in coelo, lunamque aggressus in undis,*
> *In sidus pariter saevus utrumque furit.*
> *Sub ripis latuit fors ulterioribus Echo,*
> *Audiit et vanas ludicra nympha minas:*
> *Audiit; et rabie rabiem lepidissima vindex*
> *Ulcisci statuit, parque referre pari.*
> *Ille repercussae deceptus imagine vocis,*
> *Irarum impatiens iam magis, estque magis.*
> *Reddere latratus pergit latratibus Echo;*

> *Quemque canis statuit, servat imago modum.*
> *Tandem ubi lassatae fauces, et spiritus, et vox;*
> *Defervet rabies tota, siletque canis.*
> *Et poterat siluisse prius; furor omnis ineptus,*
> *Omnisque in sese futilis ira redit.*

Notes:

1. Metre – elegiac couplets, see Appendix
2. puris … radiis – 'with clear rays'
3. Tamisis – the Thames
4. hic – adverb, 'here' (scans with a long 'i')
5. ringens – from *ringor*, 'show teeth' or 'snarl'
6. malignum – object after *vidit* – the puppy saw 'something malign'; alternatively take with *ringens* and translate as equivalent to adverb *maligne*, 'snarling spitefully'
7. solvit – 'let loose', i.e. uttered *ora proterva* – 'shameless sounds' (neuter accusative plural)
8. lunamque … lunamque – a verbal reflection imitating the actual reflection
9. sidus … utrumque – 'both planets', i.e. the two moons; the dog is *saevus*
10. fors – adverb, 'by chance'
11. ludicra – 'playful', Echo is in the mood for a game; she is the *lepidissima vindex*, 'the very charming champion'
12. rabie … rabiem, par … pari, latratus … latratibus – 'fury with fury … like for like … barks for barks', verbal echoes of Echo's echoes; *latratus* – fourth declension accusative plural
13. quemque canis statuit – 'what the dog started, the image only follows'
14. defervet – literally, 'ceases fermenting', i.e. subsides
15. in sese – anger is reflected too.

3. TO JOSEPH TAYLOR (ANTHONY ALSOP, 1670–1726)

Dubbed 'the English Horace' by David Money (see recommended reading below), Alsop was 'looked upon to be the best Writer of Lyric Verses in the World' according to the assessment of at least one of his contemporaries. After attending Westminster School, like Bourne and so many other Anglo-Latin poets of the time, Alsop went up to Oxford then led a largely uneventful life as a country parson.

He did rather unwisely champion Boyle (Oxford) against Bentley
(Cambridge) when the latter exposed Boyle's *Epistles of Phalaris* as
spurious. He was also once forced to flee the country when a woman
whom he had apparently engaged to marry sued him for breach of
promise after he married someone else.

Alsop wrote a great deal of excellent Latin poetry in a variety
of metres and on a variety of subjects, but his favourite verse form
was the Sapphic stanza and he is at his best when celebrating the
convivial delights of 'wine, women and song' in Horatian-style odes
of considerable wit and charm. Many of these odes were addressed
to friends, among whom was the lawyer Joseph Taylor, who received
this witty invitation to spend some time at Alsop's house:

Josepho Taylor

Est mihi Octobres cadus ad calendas
Natus, et pernae satis, et farinae;
Nec foco aut mensae locus, aut cubili
                    Defuit aptus.

Siquid haec ultra petis, est in anno
Forte fortuna semel et secundo
Vasculum Bacchi, quod amica, clam quaes-
                    tore, ratis fert.

Quare age, his mecum fruere, et relicta
Paululum lauta dape, ferculisque
Arte conditis, tenui salino as-
                    suesce, et inempto

Luxui. Hic vitae bona multa disces
Rusticae: hic purae data nox quieti,
Et dies transit sine lite; nulli
                    Mane clientes

Somnia abrumpent, hilarisve lusum
Vesperae; hic curis potes expeditus
Vivere; et, ni quod tua Philis absit,
                    Caetera felix.

[*Odes* Book 2.19]

Notes:

1.   Metre – Sapphics, see Appendix
2.   Octobres ... ad Calendas – i.e a cask of ale laid down on the first of October
3.   pernae ... farinae – a leg of ham and flour (bread)
4.   est in anno – understand *mihi* with *est*
5.   forte fortuna – 'as luck would have it' (*fortuna* is ablative)
6.   semel et secundo – 'from time to time', a Medieval phrase that occurs in the *Rule of St Benedict* and other Christian texts
7.   Bacchi – metonymy for wine; *vasculum* is diminutive, 'a little bottle'
8.   clam quaestore – 'without the knowledge of the customs officer'; a *quaestor* being a state treasury official in charge of the revenue
9.   fruere – imperative followed by ablative *his*
10. relicta lauta dape – ablative absolute; *lauta* is the perfect participle of *lavo* ('wash') meaning 'luxurious'
11. assuesce – imperative, followed by datives *tenui salino et inempto Luxui*, 'a plain salt cellar and luxury purchased for nothing'
12. lite – a *lis* is a lawsuit; Joseph Taylor was a lawyer
13. expeditus – followed by ablative, 'free from'
14. ni quod – 'but for the fact that'; *absit* is subjunctive because this is a hypothetical future situation.

4. EPITAPH FOR A BELOVED CAT (JOHN JORTIN, 1698–1770)

John Jortin was one of a circle of poets at Cambridge who were actively producing Latin verses at the same time as Alsop and his Oxford contemporaries. In contrast to the chatty Horatian odes of Alsop, the Cambridge poets, according to Leicester Bradner, excelled in 'the romantic descriptive ode in which the poet withdraws from society to enjoy nature in solitude, or is led to solemn reflection by the dark shades of the woods.' A younger Cambridge Latinist in this style was Thomas Gray, more famous now for his *Elegy Written in a Country Churchyard* (for a sample of Gray's Latin, see *Annus Mirabilis*, Chapter 7).

In this delightful and touching epitaph, Jortin imagines his recently deceased cat as asking Proserpina, the goddess of the underworld, for a chance to return to its beloved master just for one night in order to whisper affectionate words in his ear.

Fessa annis morboque gravi, mitissima Felis,
  Infernos tandem cogor adire lacus;
Et mihi subridens Proserpina dixit, 'Habeto
  Elysios soles, Elysiumque nemus':
'Sed, bene si merui, facilis Regina Silentum,
  Da mihi saltem una nocte redire domum,
Nocte redire domum, dominoque haec dicere in aurem,
  "Te tua fide etiam trans Styga Felis amat".'

Decessit Felis anno MDCCLVI. Vixit annos XIV, menses II, dies IV.

Notes

1.   Metre – elegiac couplets, see Appendix
2.   Felis – not genitive but an alternative spelling of nominative *Feles*; Jortin called his cat by the Latin name for cat, translate as a proper name, 'Puss'
3.   cogor – it is the cat who is narrating
4.   Proserpina – the goddess of the underworld (*infernos lacus*) mocks the unfortunate feline
5.   habeto – future imperative, '(you will) know', i.e. from this time on this is what you will have
6.   sed, bene si merui – the cat replies to Proserpina; *facilis* – 'indulgent'
7.   nocte redire domum – the repetition (*conduplicatio*) provides emphasis
8.   fide – adverb, 'faithfully'.

5. RUNNING A FEVER (WALTER SAVAGE LANDOR, 1775–1864)

A neglected literary giant whose works have fallen into near-oblivion, Landor was also one of the nineteenth century's most quixotic figures – a genius to some, eccentric madman to others. He was dogged by ill-luck throughout his life, not only in the literary sphere, and spent many years as an exile in Italy after a disastrous stint as a landowner left him in debt.

Though admired by many of his contemporaries, including Southey, Wordsworth, Coleridge and Dickens (who affectionately caricatured him as Mr Boythorn in *Bleak House*), Landor never achieved popular or critical recognition, partially as a result of his notorious irascibility – he was expelled from Oxford for shooting at a fellow student – and partially because his writing was often regarded as too obscure or highbrow. The penchant for classicism that is revealed in his *Imaginary Conversations* and *Hellenics* found its fullest expression in his copious Latin poetry, which included mythological epics, satires, political diatribes, and tender expressions of affection towards the people and places he loved. Landor probably composed more Latin verse than any British writer since the Renaissance, though little of it was either read or appreciated. In 1820, Landor's brother Robert wrote to his other brother Henry,

> I have received two or three Letters lately from Walter about some Latin Poems, which have been printed at Pisa, and sent to Longman for publication. Here is another foolish expense without the chance of sixpence in return! Who reads Latin Poems written in these days!

Of his collected *Poemata et Inscriptiones*, published in 1847, he is said to have sold just one copy. Landor lived into a weary old age, writing all the while – including more Latin verses – but was forced to spend his final years as an impoverished exile in Italy once again, after being hounded out of England by a malicious lawsuit.

Febricitans ('Running a Fever') opens with Landor paradoxically regretting that he has recovered from a fever – but the paradox is resolved when we learn he is pining for she who tended him during his illness (*adfuit ... cura*). After ennumerating her gentle ministrations, the poem closes with an appeal for the fever to return (*morbe! ... redi*), so that she might return too (*sit reditura*).

> *Febricitans*
>
> Si valeo, cuperem (fateor) caruisse medelis,
>   Et thalamum verno linquere mane piget.
> Adfuit (heu nec adest!) cuius mihi cura salutem
>   Praebuerat: clausit non reditura forem!
> At prius haud puduit nec strata obducere collo
>   Nec frontem tenero tangere flore manus,
> Nec, quam praepropero salientem sanguine venam
>   Fecerat, imposita sistere velle gena:
> Tum (quae debet adhuc) promittere praemia pacto
>   Hoc uno, patiens sim, bene iussa sequar.

> *Morbe! ferens febrem febrisque insomnia tecum,*
> *Morbe! modo infirmo sit reditura, redi.*
>
> [*Poemata et inscriptiones, Minora varia* XXXIII]

Notes:

1. Metre – elegiac couplets, see Appendix
2. cuperem – Landor wishes he hadn't taken his medicine
3. piget – impersonal, 'it is irksome (to me) to get out of bed'
4. cura – both the ministrations of his attendant and the attendant herself
5. reditura – future participle expressing purpose: 'never to return'
6. haud puduit – before she left she was not ashamed to carry out the following tasks, the infinitives *obducere, tangere, velle* and *promittere* depend on *puduit*
7. manus – genitive, 'the soft bloom of her hand'
8. salientem sanguine venam – a quote from Virgil, *Georgics* 3: *et inter / ima ferire pedis salientem sanguine venam*, 'and between the lowest parts of the foot to cut open a vein gushing with blood'; Landor's nurse had (according to the practise of the time) let some blood by opening a vein, but was not ashamed to stem the flow she had made (*quam … fecerat*) by resting her cheek (*imposita gena*) on the wound, presumably after it had been bandaged. My copy of the 1847 *Poemata et Inscriptiones* (p. 227) prints the word *venam* as *veram*, which led to some confusion for all of us when I gave this poem to my Latin evening class!
9. quae debet adhuc – she still ought to do what she promised
10. sim … sequar – jussive subjunctives, what she has told him to do
11. morbe – vocative, 'come back sickness!'
12. infirmo – dative, 'to he who is an invalid'; *modo* – adverb, 'just now, recently'.

RECOMMENDED READING

Binns, J.W. (ed.)   *The Latin Poetry of English Poets*
Routledge &·Kegan Paul

Essays on key Anglo-Latin poets, including Bourne and Landor.

Bourne, V.   *The Poetical Works*
Kessinger Publishing

A paperback facsimile reprint of the 1838 edition.

Bradner, L.   *Musae Anglicanae: A History of Anglo-Latin Poetry,* 1500–1925
The Modern Language Association of America

The primary study of this subject; though long out of print, second-hand copies can be found online.

Haan, E.   *Classical Romantic: Identity in the Latin Poetry of Vincent Bourne*
American Philosophical Society

An excellent in-depth study.

Landor, W.S.   *The Complete Latin Poetry* (2 volumes)
(ed. Binns)   Edwin Mellen Press Ltd.

Expensive and hard to find – but well worth the effort, since other sets of Landor's so-called *Complete Works* contain none of his Latin poetry.

Money, D.   *The English Horace: Anthony Alsop and the Tradition of British Latin Verse*
Oxford University Press

David Money's definitive study of Alsop.

CHAPTER 9

ANGLO-LATIN TODAY

Writing Latin poetry in the twenty-first century seems like the height of self-indulgence, not to mention folly. As we saw in the previous chapter, even in the nineteenth century Walter Savage Landor was ridiculed for his fondness for Latin versifying – and that in an age when every educated person could read Latin with relative ease. In a time when only a privileged minority are given the opportunity to encounter Latin at school, Latin composition today seems like an even more futile endeavour.

But if this book has achieved nothing else I hope it has impressed upon the reader that Latin has always been a vital element in the literary and social history of Britain. The idea that Latin is nothing more than the dead language of the long-dead Roman Empire is false; Latin thrived in Britain until very recent times and made a significant contribution to our culture. For a contemporary British writer, then, composing Latin can be a way of engaging (or re-engaging) not only with the literature and culture of Rome, but also with our own heritage too.

There are caveats: the stultifiying practice of 'Prose Comp' in schools – usually painfully (re)creating sentences in the style of Caesar's military memoirs – has rightly led to the impression that writing Latin is a dreary and utterly pointless classrooom drill. Similarly, the habit of paraphrasing vernacular works – a habit that began as far back as the Renaissance – has led to Latin poetry becoming progressively more 'academic', an exercise in making neat Classical verses out of English texts instead of creating original new work.

Another Renaissance hangover, the close imitation of Classical models, has also proved an obstacle to the continuance of a living tradition of Latin verse; it seems that only those (usually professional academics) who have devoted years to a close study of Roman literature can possibly attempt to compose their own imitations. Indeed so – but why imitate in the first place? Why not say something original in words that are your own, not filtered through Virgil or Horace? The spurious requirement that new Latin verse should conform to the style and practice of Roman writers is at least as silly as requiring all modern English poetry to be rigidly Shakespearian.

To write Latin poetry (or prose for that matter) does not have to mean copying Classical examplars and worrying whether every word and every construction is sanctioned by the usage of antiquity. The ability to compose Latin verse in Classically correct quantitative metres is a fine achievement, but it is not the only way to do it. Perhaps in order for Latin poetry to experience any sort of revival a little of the medieval spirit is now required – I mean the freedom to express contemporary thought in a modern idiom. That is what the poets of the *Carmina Burana* collection did – their Latin was adapted to their own times and usages – so why can't we do the same?

Although the examples that follow are all explicitly Classical in form, that does not mean you, the reader – and budding Latin poet – need to follow the same route. Have a go at writing something in Latin, feel free to experiment, don't worry about imitating others, and above all don't be afraid to follow where your Latin Muse leads you.

CONTEMPORARY LATIN POETRY ONLINE

Latinised Hymns by Mark Mortimer – some 300 hymns translated into Latin and preserving the same metre and rhyme scheme as the originals:
http://www.latinisedhymns.org.uk/

Edward Lear Limericks and other pieces translated into Latin by Timothy Adès:
http://colecizj.easyvserver.com/vcb8cove.htm

Contemporary Latin Poetry – a website featuring various Latin poets from Europe and the USA:
http://suberic.net/~marc/latinpoetry.html

Hymnus Latinus Europae – the unofficial anthem of the European Union, sung to the tune of 'Ode to Joy':
http://www.hymnus-europae.at/

See also the *Society for Neo-Latin Studies*
http://www2.warwick.ac.uk/fac/arts/ren/snls/

There is also a Facebook group called *Carmina Latina: Contemporary Latin Poetry*, for anyone who wants to post examples of their own compositions.

1. ADVICE FOR A BEGINNER (FRANK LELIÈVRE)

Frank Lelièvre was Professor of Classics at Magee College in Londonderry and then at the University of Ulster in Coleraine. He first began to write Latin poetry while lecturing at Bedford College, London in the late 1940s, but then didn't write anything more until after his retirement. He has published three volumes, subtitled 'Latin poems in various metres', which include both translations from English originals and new Latin poems. These are *Across Bin Brook* (1992, with H.H. Huxley), *Serus Vindemitor* (1995) and *Rarae Uvae* (2009).

The Alcaic ode *For a Beginner* is taken with the author's kind permission from *Across Bin Brook*. Here Professor Lelièvre offers some comforting words of advice for all those who wish to take up the challenge of composing their own Latin verses.

For a Beginner

Perstare, credo, Musa suos iubet,
utcumque chordis dulcisonos negat
cantus et, exoptata quamvis,
pervigilem refugit lucernam.

nascentis ipso germine flos rosae
celatur: ignem dura tegit silex:
et Terra fulgorem smaragdi
condidit interiore saxo.

at pertinacem, sera licet, virum
ditare gaudet: non silicis latet
scintilla percussae, nec omni
tempore flos Veneris moratur.

tu perge tantum, namque potes, modis
verba experiri convenientia.
te Musa quaerentem docebit
mente nova reparare carmen.

© Frank Lelièvre

Notes:

1. Metre – Alcaics, see Appendix
2. perstare – 'to keep trying'; *suos* – 'her own followers', i.e. would-be poets; *credo* – parenthetical, 'I reckon'
3. utcumque – 'even though she with olds (*negat*) sweet-sounding songs from our strings (*chordis*)'; *chordis* is a Horatian poetical conceit, picturing the would-be poet as plucking the strings of a cithara or lyre
4. refugit – 'she shuns our night-long labours (*pervigilem lucernam*)'; the Muse bids us keep trying even though she seems to have deserted us
5. nascentis ... saxo – the second stanza provides us with some metaphorical examples of hidden potential: the seed which conceals the rose, flint's ability to make fire, the brilliance (*fulgor*) of the emerald (*smaragdus*) hidden in earth's deepest rock
6. sera licet – 'although tardily'; the Muse loves to enrich he who perseveres (*pertinacem virum*)
7. non silicis ... moratur – returning to the metaphors of the previous stanza, the spark of the struck flint (*silicis percussae*), the flower of Love (*Veneris*) show themselves eventually
8. tu perge – imperative, addressing the tiro poet; *tantum*, 'at any rate'; *experiri* – deponent infinitive: 'carry on experimenting in whatever way you can'
9. quaerentem – 'while you are learning'
10. mente nova – 'with a new understanding'; the more you experiment the better your song (*carmen*) will become.

2. HAY FEVER (DAVID MONEY)

Professor David Money of Cambridge University is an expert on Neo-Latin poetry as well as a prolific Latin poet himself. His book *The English Horace* is both a biography of Anthony Alsop (Chapter 8) and a complete edition of Alsop's poetry; it is also an engaging survey of much other Anglo-Latin verse. Money's own Latin compositions have appeared in journals and anthologies, and he has even set up his own imprint, Bringfield's Head Press, to encourage the writing and publication of Latin verses.

Febris aestiva was first printed in the Neo-Latin anthology *Alaudae*, edited by A.E. Radke (2004) and is reprinted here by kind permission of the author.

Bringfield's Head Press
https://perswww.kuleuven.be/~u0044197/BHP/

David Money's private press has already published two anthologies of
new Latin: *Ramillies: A Commemoration in Prose and Verse of the 300th
Anniversary of the Battle of Ramillies*, and *1708: Oudenarde and Lille*.

Febris aestiva, sive foenisecis

Sternuere est faustum (priscorum rite parentum)
   Significare potest omen adesse bonum.
Ergo ultra meritam sortem sum saepe beatus:
   Auspiciis tantis ominibusque fruor.
Vexat enim nares foenum, cum flore venusto,
   Nasum per campos innocua herba nocet.
Solvere vexando mucum corpuscula certant,
   Phlegmatis ut rapidi flumine cuncta ruant.
Contineo strepitum, rabidis dum naribus actus
   Sternuo, seu viso sternuo sole simul.
Finis erit? Dubium est, longoque haeremus hiatu -
   Stern- stern- stern- stern- stern- sternuimusque iterum.
Sternutamentum sternutamenta sequuntur
   Plura (moram spernunt) continua serie.
Quae requies? Oculos purgo, purgoque lavando
   Nasum ut sit gelidae dulce levamen aquae.
Multa mihi placeant aestate: at febris amorem
   Foenisecis placidum saepe fragore fugat.

© David Money

Notes:

1. Metre – elegiac couplets, see Appendix
2. foenisecis – or *faenisecis*, genitive of *faenisex*, 'a mower, hay-cutter'
3. sternuere – 'sneezing'
4. rite – adverb, 'according to the rites of'
5. ultra meritam sortem – 'more than is my fair share'
6. fruor – takes the ablative, hence *auspiciis … ominibus*, 'portents and
    omens'

7.   foenum – or *faenum*, 'hay'

8.   corpuscula – 'tiny particles', i.e. the pollen 'strive (*certant*) by constant harrying (gerund *vexando*) to loosen mucus'

9.   phlegmatis – genitive of *phlegma*, after *cuncta* – 'all (of) the phlegm'; *ut … ruant* – result clause, 'so that it runs down'

10. actus – participle of *ago*, here = 'having drawn breath'

11. viso … sole – ablative absolute, literally: 'with the sun having been seen'

12. haeremus – plural for singular, 'I come to a standstill with mouth gaping wide'; the 'h' of *hiatu* does not count for scansion

13. stern-stern – the repetition cleverly occupies the first half of the pentameter; Money uses not only repetition but also alliteration and assonance to achieve a comical effect here and in the next line

14. lavando – gerund, 'by washing'

15. ut sit – result clause, 'to have the sweet relief of cold water'

16. fragore – 'with a crash', i.e. the noise of sneezing dispels the peace and quiet.

3. A THANK YOU (ARMAND D'ANJOUR)

Armand D'Anjour is Tutor in Classics at Jesus College, Oxford. He was taught to write Latin and Greek verse at Eton and went on to win the Chancellor's Latin Verse Prize at Oxford in 1980. Inspired by the examples of Catullus and Martial he particularly enjoys writing elegiac epigrams, which he regards as an ideal vehicle for erudite wit. Since composing a Pindaric Ode for the Athens Olympics 2004, he has often been asked to supply verses in both Latin and Greek. He advocates reintroducing Latin verse composition into the school curriculum as the best way of teaching students how Latin poetry works.

This witty thank you note is reprinted with the author's kind permission.

> *Assidua adiutrix, viginti quinque per annos*
> *   hic veterum data sunt scripta probanda tibi;*
> *inspiciens chartas, seu Graece sive Latine,*
> *   e scriptis poteras omne fugare malum,*
> *semper ut exactam mendis maculisque remotis*
> *   rem faceres: grates hic tibi versus agat.*

Notes:

1. Metre – elegiac couplets, see Appendix
2. adiutrix – the *–trix* ending is the feminine of *–tor*
3. veterum – genitive plural after *scripta*, 'of things belonging to the past' i.e. the papers written by members of the Classics department; *probanda* – gerundive, 'to be approved'
4. omne fugare malum – she corrected every mistake
5. ut … faceres – result clause, she made the *chartas* accurate (*exactam*)
6. mendis maculisque remotis – ablative absolute, 'with faults and blemishes removed'
7. grates … agat – *grates agere* is 'to give thanks'; *hic versus* – this poem.

4. ON COOMBE HILL (MARK WALKER)

A short piece in celebration of Coombe Hill on the Chiltern ridge in Buckinghamshire not far from my home – a delightful place for walking with the dog, enjoying the views across Aylesbury Vale, eating picnics and flying kites.

In Colle Concavo Ambulans

Amoena moles, optimi loci palmam
Dedi tibi, dum prata per tua errabam:
Ubique palor cum caniculo, passim
Cuniculosas ille per vias currens
Comesque laetus. Hic columna nunc sursum,
Stilus superbus imminens super campis
Quibus sonorum tinnule sonat templum.
Renidet aestas: murmurat iocosa aura
Per arboresque vepribus susurratve,
Crescitve ventus aptus ad volandumque
ventosa vela: subvolant simul corda,
Cadit deorsum in stragulis agris cura.

Notes:

1. Metre – scazons or 'limping' iambics, see Appendix
2. concavo – 'Coombe' is an old English word meaning 'hollow'
3. amoena – the traditional epithet to describe natural beauty

4. tua errabam – the final 'a' of *tua* is elided, *tu(a) errabam*; similarly *iocos(a) aura* in line eight

5. caniculo – 'little dog', see also the poem *Plato Mi* in *Annus Mirabilis*; note alliteration with *cuniculosas … currens*

6. columna – the Boer war memorial at the summit of Coombe Hill, overlooking the Prime Minister's residence at Chequers, and commanding views across Wendover, Aylesbury and into Oxfordshire

7. quibus – 'in which', i.e. the *campis*

8. tinnule – adverb, 'clangingly'; the *templum* is the church of St Peter and St Paul in Ellesborough, whose bells can be heard distinctly from the hill above

9. aptus – followed by *ad* + gerund *volandum* (from *volo, volare*)

10. vela – in this context, 'kites'; the Chiltern ridge is exposed to winds, which are pleasingly cool in summer making Coombe Hill perfect for kite-flying

11. stragulis agris – 'patchwork fields', the classic English countryside spread out below like a knitted quilt

12. cura – the key word delayed to the end.

5. JOYCE (FRANK LELIÈVRE)

I leave the last word to Frank Lelièvre and this touching elegy from *Rarae Uvae*:

> Omnia mortis erunt: rapuit mors Gaudia nostra,
>   nec queror: invalidae non ea dura venit.
> dura tamen quod me cara cum coniuge iunctum
>   nocte sub aeterna non requiesse sinit.

© Frank Lelièvre

Notes:

1. Metre – elegiac couplets, see Appendix

2. mortis erunt – 'will partake of death'

3. Gaudia – a pun on his wife's name ('Joy')

4. dura tamen – but it is a hardship for the one left behind.

RECOMMENDED READING

Lelièvre, F.

Across Bin Brook (with H.H. Huxley) and
Serus Vindemitor
Privately published
Rarae Uvae
Available from Lulu.com

Money. D. et al.

Ramillies: A Commemoration in Prose and Verse of the 300th Anniversary of the Battle of Ramillies
Bringfield's Head Press

Radke, A. E (ed.)

Alaudae (anthology of new Latin verse)
Georg Olms Verlag

ENGLISH TRANSLATIONS

Pedantically literal, for reference only

Chapter I

I. THE ROMANS FORCE A LANDING ON BRITISH SOIL (CAESAR)

And while our soldiers were hesitating, especially because of the depth of the sea, he who was carrying the eagle of the tenth legion, having called the gods to witness that this matter should turn out fortunately for the legion, said 'Jump down, soldiers, unless you wish to abandon the eagle to the enemy; I at any rate will have discharged my duty to the state and to my general.' When he had said this with a loud voice, he flung himself from the ship and began to carry the eagle towards the enemy. Then our men encouraging each other, lest such a great disgrace should be incurred, leapt all together from the ship. When the troops on the nearest ships had seen them, having followed closely after they drew near to the enemy.

The battle was fought keenly by both sides. Our men, however, because they were able neither to keep ranks nor to get a firm footing nor to follow the standards, and any man from any ship attached himself to whatever standards he had chanced upon, were greatly thrown into confusion; the enemy indeed, since they were familiar with all the shallows, when they had observed from the shore some of our men departing one by one from the ship, having spurred on their horses attacked our encumbered men, many crowded around a few, others were throwing missiles from the open flank against all our men. When Caesar noticed this, he ordered the boats of the warships, likewise the scouting ships, to be filled up with soldiers and, when he caught sight of those in distress, he sent reinforcements to them. Our men, as soon as they stood on dry land, with all their comrades following after, attacked the enemy and put them to flight; but they were not able to follow further, because the cavalry [in its ships] had not been able to maintain a course and reach the island. In this one thing Caesar lacked his former fortune.

2. CLAUDIUS CONQUERS BRITAIN (SUETONIUS)

He undertook one expedition in all and that unimpressive. When after triumphal ornaments had been decreed to him by the Senate he decided that the award was too slight for his imperial majesty and desired the glory of a proper triumph, he selected as the most likely place from which he could acquire it Britain, which had not been attempted by anyone after the Divine Julius and was then in an uproar because the deserters had not been handed back. While he was sailing there from the vicinity of Ostia, he was twice almost sunk by a violent circular wind in the vicinity of Liguria beside the Stoechadae islands. Thence with the journey overland having been completed from Massilia up to Gesoriacum from there he crossed over and without any battle or bloodshed having received in surrender part of the island within the briefest span of days he returned to Rome in the sixth month after he had set out and celebrated a triumph with the greatest pomp.

3. EARLY BRITISH INSCRIPTIONS

(a)   Tiberius Claudius Caesar Augustus Pontifex Maximus, holder of tribunican power nine times, hailed as supreme leader 16 times, in commemoration of his victory over the Britons.

(b)   For the safety of the Divine House, by the authority of Tiberius Claudius Cogidubnus, Great King of Britain, the college of artificers and its members provided at their own expense this temple to Neptune and Minerva, with [?Clemens] son of Pudentinus making a donation of the land.

(c)   To the departed spirit of Gaius Julius, son of Gaius, Alpinus Classicianus of the Fabian voting tribe ... Procurator of the province of Britain, Julia Pacata, daughter of Indus ... his [?unhappy] wife set this up.

(d)   Arepo the Sower guides the wheels with effort [one possibility only]

4. THE ROMANS LEAVE FOREVER (GILDAS)

Thus the Romans, declaring to Britain that by no means could they be harassed any longer by such troublesome expeditions, and on account of the unwarlike and wandering bandits, who had been branded as infamous by the Romans, could such a great and exceptional army be worn out by land and sea; but rather that Britain unaided, by becoming accustomed to arms and fighting bravely, should lay claim to its subsistence land, wives, children and – what is greater than these – freedom and life with all its strength and by no means be divided up by stronger nations, unless by its own sloth and lethargy, that it should stretch forth its hands in no way unarmed to be bound in chains, but equipped with shields, swords and spears and readily inclined to slaughter, thus they were recommending, and because they thought to add something of benefit to the people they were abandoning, they by private and public expense, with the miserable natives joining them, build a level wall unlike the other in the accustomed manner of a brick structure, with its route from sea to sea having been fixed between cities which in that same place by chance had been established on account of fear of the enemy; they give courageous advice to the frightened people, and leave behind patterns for fabricating arms. On the shore of the ocean, too, facing to the south, on which their ships are placed, and because from that direction the wild savage beasts are feared, they establish towers at intervals for the purpose of surveying the sea, and say farewell, so to speak, never to return.

Chapter 2

1. THE ARRIVAL OF THE ANGLO-SAXONS (BEDE)

Then unexpectedly having entered into a treaty with the Picts, whom they had now by waging war driven back a long way, they began to turn their arms against their allies; and at first indeed they compelled them to supply provisions to them in greater abundance, and seeking an opportunity for a quarrel, they publicly declared that unless more profusely a supply of foodstuffs was given to them, they would, having broken their treaty, devastate every place in the island; and by no means less actively did they follow up their threats with actions. At any rate, as I shall briefly relate, the fire ignited by the hands of the pagans, which exacted the righteous retribution of God for the crimes of the people, was not inferior to that which once having been kindled by the Chaldeans consumed the walls of Jerusalem, or rather all of its buildings. For with the impious conqueror behaving in the same way here as well, rather by the management of the just Judge, depopulating each of the nearest cities and fields, from the eastern sea all the way to the western, with nothing to prevent him, he continued his destruction, and covered almost the entire surface of the ruined island. Public buildings as well as private ones collapsed, everywhere priests were slaughtered beside their altars, bishops along with the people without any respect for their office, were consumed alike by fire and sword; nor was there anyone who might deliver for burial those cruelly murdered. And so some from among the pitiful remnants having been seized in the mountains, were slain in heaps; others worn out by hunger coming forward surrendered themselves to the enemy, in return for receiving a supply of food they were to endure eternal servitude, if they were not immediately slaughtered that is; some in mourning sought regions across the sea; others remaining in their homeland filled with anxiety lived a life of poverty in the mountains, the forests or among harsh rocks, always feeling apprehensive.

But when the enemy army, having exterminated and dispersed the natives of the islands, returned home, they began by degrees to regain their strength and courage, and emerging from their hiding-places, where they had hidden themselves, and by unanimous consent they were praying for heavenly help, that they not be altogether obliterated to the point of extermination. They took at that time as their leader Ambrosius Aurelianus, a mild man, who alone of the Roman race by chance had survived the aforementioned storm, though his parents who bore the name and insignia of royalty were killed in it. With him as their leader, therefore, the Britons took courage, and summoning the victors to battle they themselves, being favoured by God, received the victory; and from that time at one moment the natives at another the enemy conquered, up to the year of the siege of Mount Badon, when they gave not the least slaughter to that enemy, in about the forty-fourth year after their arrival in Britain.

2. THE TYRANNICAL RULERS OF BRITAIN (GILDAS)

Britain has kings, but they are tyrants; it has judges, but they are ungodly; they often plunder and intimidate, but they are free from blame; they are defenders and advocates, but they are guilty and robbers; they have many wives, but they consort with prostitutes and are adulterers; repeatedly they take oaths, but they are perjurers; they make vows, and almost continually tell lies; they are war-mongers, but makers of civil and unjust wars; some earnestly pursue thieves throughout the country, and yet those, who sit at table with them, are bandits and they not only love them but also reward them; they are generous givers of alms, but on the other hand they heap up a vast mountain of crimes; they sit on the seat in order to pass judgement, but rarely do they require the standard of an impartial trial; they despise the blameless and the humble; they praise to the stars as much as they can the arrogant and bloodthirsty, their fellow murderers and adulterers, if fate, so it is said, will endure it, the enemies of God, those who in his very name certainly ought to be destroyed; they have many vanquished foes in their prisons, whom they crush by a deceit of theirs rather than their own due weighing them down with chains; and they detain them by taking an oath on the altars, and despise those same a little while later as if they were mud-covered stones.

3. LADY GODIVA (ROGER OF WENDOVER)

But Godiva the countess and lover of the mother of God, endeavouring to free the village of Coventry from the heavy burden of the toll, often asked her husband the count with a great many prayers, in consideration of Jesus Christ and his mother to release the village from the above-mentioned servitude and from other troublesome taxes; and when the count would reproach her, that without good reason she was demanding something detrimental to him, without further ado he forbade her to approach him concerning this matter any more. On the contrary she, led by a womanly stubbornness, incessantly exasperating her husband about the aforementioned matters, received this reply from him: 'Mount,' he said, 'your horse naked and cross the village market-place from the beginning right to the end, with the people gathered round, and when you return, you will obtain what you demand.' To whom Godiva replying said, 'And, if I am willing, will you give me permission?' To her he said, 'I will.' Then the countess beloved by God accompanied by two soldiers, naked, as was said above, mounting her horse let down the hair from her head and loosened the curls and hence she concealed her whole body, and passing through the market she was seen by no one, though with her lovely white legs visible, she completed the journey, and rejoicing returned to her husband, who was marvelling at this deed, and that which she had sought she obtained; for count Leofric, freeing the village of Coventry and its inhabitants from the aforesaid servitude, confirmed in writing what he had done.

4. THE BATTLE OF HASTINGS (WILLIAM OF MALMESBURY)

And so on both sides the proud commanders draw up their battle lines, each according to his native usage: the English, as we have been told, spending the whole sleepless night in singing and drinking, in the morning without hesitation advance against the enemy: all the infantry with double-bladed axes, a tortoise formation of shields having been joined together in front of them, they will make an impenetrable formation; which undoubtedly on that day might have been their salvation, if the Normans by a pretended flight had not scattered the companies which were according to their custom densely packed. The King himself on foot was standing next to the standard with his brothers, so that, having been made an equal in their communal peril, no one would consider flight. After his victory, William sent to the Pope that standard, which was in the shape of a fighting man, woven with lavish skill from gold and precious gems.

On the opposite side, the Normans giving the whole night to the confession of their sins, in the morning they partake of the Lord's body. The infantry with their bows and arrows defend the front row, the cavalry having been separated into wings take position behind. The general, with tranquil countenance and in a bright voice proclaiming that since their cause was the more righteous God will be with them, demanded his armour: and soon from the confusion of his attendants having put on his cuirass upside down, he made good a cause for laughter saying, 'The strength of my Dukedom will be turned into a kingdom.' Then having begun the song of Roland so that the martial example of that man might rouse those who were about to fight, and having invoked the aid of God, battle was joined and fought fiercely, with neither side yielding until late in the day. Having ascertained this, William indicated to his men to withdraw themselves from the camp by a pretended retreat. By this stratagem, the formation of the English, having been broken so as to cut down the fleeing enemy from the rear, hastened its own demise. For the Normans, having turned round with their ranks faced about, attack the scattered troops, and force them to flee. Thus tricked by ingenuity, they deserved an honourable death in return for the avenging of their native country: nor however did they lack their own vengeance, but that, repeatedly halting, they made conspicuous heaps of slaughter among those who were following them; for, having occupied a hill, they threw down into the valley the Normans who inflamed by zeal were struggling vigorously towards the higher position, and with little trouble casting javelins and rolling stones onto those below, they rout all without exception. Again avoiding a certain steep ditch by a route that was short and familiar to them, they trampled underfoot there so many of the enemy, that with the heap of corpses they made [the ditch] level with the surface of the field. This toing and froing carried on, now with these now with the others prevailing, as long as the life of Harold was an obstacle; but when he fell with his skull pierced by the flight of an arrow, the flight of the English was uninterrupted until night. In that place the courage of both leaders shone forth.

5. THE SIGNING OF THE MAGNA CARTA (MATTHEW PARIS)

Freedoms are granted deceitfully and peace is made, but hateful. But the King discerning that he now had been deserted by almost everyone, began to be extremely frightened for himself, and, having conceived an inexorable hatred against them, he pretended deceitfully that he wished to make peace at the appointed time, so that, when he had risen up more strongly afterwards, he could avenge himself more severely against the dispersed armies, and he who had not been able to rage against all, could do so more cautiously against each in turn. Therefore sending to them William Mareschal, Earl of Pembroke, with certain others worthy of his trust, he announced to them in friendly manner, that for the sake of peace and the pride of his kingdom and with an accompanying promise of his sincerity, he granted to them the freedoms which they were seeking. So they having rejoiced, and revived by a false joy, appointed the day for him to come to face them for a conference, in a field between Staines and Windelsham, on the 15th day of June. When they had arrived there, the king in friendly manner conceded to the barons their demands, and signed the charter. But afterwards King John, brooding over something in his heart, by his own volition added in addition to all the freedoms and laws demanded by the barons almost as if it were superfluous:

'But since for God and for the amendment of our kingdom, and for the sake of better calming the discord which has arisen between us and our barons, we have granted all these things, wishing that they are established untouched and stable, we assert and grant to them the security written below, namely that the barons should appoint 25 barons from the kingdom, whom they have chosen, who ought with all their might to observe, to hold, and to cause to be observed the peace and freedoms, which we have granted to them, and confirmed by this our present charter, that is to say that, if we or our justiciar in some way do wrong towards someone, or transgress some of the articles and that wrong has been pointed out to four of the barons from the 25, those four shall approach us or our justiciar, if we are out of the kingdom, laying before us the deviation, they shall ask that without delay we see to it that it is corrected. But if we do not correct that deviation within the period of 40 days, reckoned from the time which it was pointed out, the aforementioned four barons shall refer that cause to the remainder of the 25 barons, and those with the community of the whole land shall detain and oppress us in every way they can, until it has been corrected according to their arbitration; saving our person, and of the queen and our children. And when it has been corrected, they shall exert themselves for us, as they did before.'

Chapter 3

1. MERLIN HELPS UTHERPENDRAGON (GEOFFREY OF MONMOUTH)

Having been summoned forthwith Merlin, when he stood in the presence of the king, was ordered to give his advice as to how the king could satisfy his desire for Igraine. Having learnt of the anxiety which the king was suffering because of her, he was moved by his exceedingly great love and said, 'In order for you to obtain your wish you must make use of methods new and unheard-of in your age. By my medicines I know how to give you the appearance of Gorlois, so that you will seem to be him in every respect. And so if you comply I will make you resemble him; and Ulfin likewise his companion Jordan of Tintagel. And having taken on another appearance I will be the third, and you will be able to approach the citadel and Igraine in safety, and to have admittance.' And so the king complied, and gave his attention diligently. At last with the siege having been entrusted to his companions, he entrusted himself to Merlin's medicines, and was transformed into the appearance of Gorlois. And Ulfin was changed into Jordan, Merlin into Britaelis, so that what they had been was obvious to no one: next they approached the road to Tintagel, and with the twilight they came to the citadel. When it was announced to the gatekeeper that his leader was coming earlier than expected, the gates were opened, and the men were admitted. For who else could have approached, when Gorlois himself was thought to have been present? And so the king stayed the whole night with Igraine and by love-making achieved what he had desired for himself. For he had deceived her by the disguise which he had assumed; he had also deceived her by fictitious speeches, which he was making up in high style. For he said that he had left the besieged city to make arrangements for her who was so beloved and for the city; for which reason she being trustful denied him nothing that he was demanding. And so on this same night she conceived the most celebrated Arthur, who subsequently deserved by his remarkable virtue to be celebrated.

2. ARTHUR'S BATTLES (NENNIUS)

In that time the Saxons were growing strong in a multitude and were expanding in Britain. But with the death of Hengist his son Octha crossed from the northern part of Britain to the kingdom of Kent and from him arose the kings of Kent. Then Arthur fought against them in those days with the kings of the Britons, but he himself was the leader of the battles. The first battle was in the mouth of the river which is called Glein. The second and third and fourth and fifth were on the banks of another river which is called Douglas and is in the region of Linnuis. The sixth battle was on the banks of the river which is called Bassas. The seventh battle was in the Caldeonian forest, that is 'the battle of the Caledonian Forest'. The eighth battle was in the castle of Guinnion, in which Arthur carried the image of the holy Mary the perpetual virgin on his shield and the pagans were put to flight on that day and there was great slaughter over them through the virtue of our lord Jesus Christ and through the virtue of the holy Mary his mother. The ninth battle was fought in the city of Legion. He fought the tenth battle on the shore of the river which is called Tryfrwyd. The eleventh battle was undertaken on the mount which is called Agned. The twelfth battle was on mount Badon, in which fell in one day nine hundred and sixty men by one attack of Arthur; and no one felled them except he alone, and in all battles he showed himself the victor.

3. THE MADNESS OF MERLIN (GEOFFREY OF MONMOUTH)

And [Merlin] mourns the men nor does he cease to pour out tears, he sprinkled his hair with dust and ripped off his clothes and lying flat on the ground he rolls now this way now that. Peredur comforts him, as do the nobles and dukes, neither does he wish to be comforted nor endure their supplicatory words. By now he had lamented for three days entire and had refused food, such great grief had consumed him. From that time on, after he had filled the air with so many and such great laments, he suffered a new madness and stealthily withdrew and fled to the woods, nor does he wish to be seen while fleeing, and he enters the forest and rejoices to skulk beneath the ash trees and marvels at the beasts grazing on the grass of the glade; now he follows them, now he passes by them at a run. He consumes the roots of plants, he consumes the plants, he consumes the fruit of the trees and the blackberries from the bramble bush; he becomes a man of the woods as though devoted to the woods. From then on during the whole summer he was discovered by no one and forgetful of himself and of his own kindred he hid himself in the woods, clothed in the manner of a wild beast. But when winter came and it had carried off the plants and all the fruits of the trees and he could not enjoy what he had, he poured forth such complaints as these in a pitiable voice: 'O Christ God of heaven, what shall I do? In which part of the earth will I be able to remain since there is nothing here that I can eat?'

4. THE GREATNESS OF ARTHUR (JOSEPH OF EXETER)

Thence Arthur by destined birth and distinguished good fortune became famous, the flower of kings, whose deeds though astonishing shone no less, which was a source of pleasure to the ears and in the people's applause he was wholly honey-sweet. Regard whomever came before: the renown of monarchs commends Alexander; Roman writings speak of the triumphs of Caesars; having subdued monsters, glory exalts Hercules. But neither do hazels equal the pine, nor stars the sun: scroll through Latin and Greek annals, the olden days did not know his like, future days will exhibit no equal. He surpasses all kings, better alone than all predecessors, and greater than those to come.

5. THE DEATH OF ARTHUR (GEOFFREY OF MONMOUTH)

And so with the commanders on both sides exhorting their own men, in a sudden charge the battle lines collided, and with the battle started they were striving to make numerous blows connect. Then there was on both sides such great slaughter, such groans of the dying, such fury of the attackers, as is both distressing and difficult to describe. For everywhere men were inflicting wounds and were being wounded, they were killing and being killed. But after they had spent the greater part of the day in this manner, at last Arthur with one division, in which he had placed 6,660 men, charged toward that squadron where he knew that Mordred was, and by opening a path with their swords, he penetrated it, and heaped up the grimmest slaughter. For that execrable traitor fell, and many thousands with him. However the rest did not flee because of his death, but gathering from every camp, as far as their boldness allowed attempted to resist. Thus the most dreadful fighting was perpetrated among them, in which almost all the leaders who had been present on both sides fell along with their own men. For on Mordred's side fell: Cheldric, Elaf, Egbric, Bunig, all Saxons; Gillapatria, Gillamor, Gislafel,

Gillarvus, Irishmen; the Scots and the Picts, too, with almost all those among them were diminished. But on Arthur's side: Olbrict king of Norway, Aschil king of Denmark, Cadmor Limenic, Cassivellanus, together with many thousands of their own men and as many Britons as the other nations which he had brought with him. But the famous king Arthur too was mortally wounded, who having been conveyed from that place to the island of Avalon in order to heal his wounds, yielded the crown of Britain to his cousin Constantine, son of Cador duke of Cornwall, in the 542nd year after the incarnation of the Lord.

6. ARTHUR'S BONES (GERALD OF WALES)

But his [Arthur's] body, which the tales had alleged was in the end like something imaginary, and was moved through the spirit so to speak to far away places, and nor was it liable to death, was found in our own day at Glastonbury, between two stone pyramids which once stood in the sacred cemetery, deeply hidden in the earth by a hollow oak and designated by marvellous signs and almost miraculous ones at that, and it was moved into the church with honour and properly entrusted to a marble tomb. And there a leaden cross – with a stone placed not above as is customary in our day but rather fastened to the lower side, which we have also seen, for we have touched the inscribed letters which are neither raised nor standing out, but facing more inwards to the stone – preserved [these words]: 'Here lies buried the famous king Arthur with Guinevere his second wife in the island of Avalon.'

But many notable things happened here; for he had two wives, of whom the last had been buried with him, and her bones were found together with the bones of her husband, but separated in this way, that two parts of the tomb, namely those towards the head, had been assigned to contain the bones of the man, but the third towards the feet contained set apart the woman's bones; and there was found a blonde lock of woman's hair with its original quality and colour, which when a certain monk eagerly grabbed it in his hand and lifted it up, the whole immediately crumbled into dust.

What is now called Glastonbury, in olden times was called the island of Avalon. For it is almost an island entirely covered with marshes, whence it was called in the British language 'Inis Avallon', that is the apple-bearing island. For that place formerly abounded in apples, which are called 'aval' in the British tongue. And whence Morgan, the noble matron and leader of those parts, and also related by blood to king Arthur, carried Arthur after the battle of Camlan to the island which is now called Glastonia for the purpose of healing his wounds. It had also been formerly called in British 'Inis gutrin', that is, the glass island; from which designation the Saxons coming afterwards referred to that place as 'Glastingeburi'. For 'Glas' in their tongue means glass, and 'buri' a settlement which is called a city.

It must also be known that the bones of Arthur's body which were discovered were so large, that this remark of the poet was able to be seen to have been fulfilled: 'And he will marvel at great bones from the disinterred tombs'. For the bone of his shin having been placed alongside the shin of the tallest man of that place, whom the abbot pointed out to us, and fixed on the ground next to his foot, extended itself further than three fingers beyond his knee. The bone of his head, too, was capacious and thick to the point of being, as it were, a prodigy or wonder, so much so that the space between the eyebrows and between the eyes contained to a great extent the full extent of a hand's width. But ten wounds or more were apparent on this bone, all of which had knitted together into a solid scar, except one greater than all of the rest, which had made a large hole and which alone seemed to have been lethal.

Chapter 4

1. THE MARTYRDOM OF ST ALBAN (BEDE)

And when he was being led to death, he came to a river by which with its very swift motion the town was separated from the area where he was to be slain; and he saw there a great multitude of people of both sexes, of varying circumstance and age, which without doubt was called by a divine prompting to escort the most blessed confessor and martyr and so occupied the bridge of that river that it was hardly able to cross within the space of that evening. Finally after almost everyone had left, the judge remained in the city without an escort. Therefore St Alban who had a burning in his heart to attain martyrdom more swiftly approached the torrent and directing his eyes to heaven, with the river channel having dried up on the spot, he saw that its flow had ceased and that a path had been given to his footsteps. When among others the executioner himself, who was going to kill him, had seen this, he hurried to meet him [Alban] at the appointed place of death where he had come, undoubtedly prompted by a divine instigation, and having flung down the sword, which he had held drawn, at his feet he threw himself down, much desiring that with the martyr or in place of the martyr, whom he was ordered to kill, rather he himself deserved to be killed.

While, therefore, from being a persecutor he became a colleague of truth and faith, and with the sword lying cast down there remained among the executioners a just hesitation, the most reverend confessor of God together with the crowd ascended the hill; which being opportunely fertile, most fittingly pleasant, was situated almost 500 feet from the place of execution, painted – rather always clothed – with the varied flowers of plants; on which there is nothing suddenly dangerous nor precipitous nor steep, whose sides sloping away in all directions nature levels off in the manner of a plain, a worthy place indeed by its innate appearance of beauty, for a long time past reappearing, to have been consecrated by the blood of the blessed martyr. On its summit, then, St Alban asked that he would be given water by God and immediately, with its course confined, arose an everlasting spring before his feet, so that everyone understood that even a stream had flowed in compliance with the wishes of the martyr, for nor is it possible that the martyr, who had left no water in the river, would have sought water on the dry summit of the hill, unless he saw that it was advantageous. The river indeed, with its service done and its duty completed, leaving this testimony of its obedience, returned to its natural state.

And so having been beheaded the most courageous martyr at that moment received the crown of life which God promised to those who love him. But he who laid impious hands on his neck was not permitted to rejoice after his death; for his eyes fell on the ground together with the head of the blessed martyr. Then that soldier was also beheaded there who, previously warned by a heavenly sign, refused to kill the holy confessor of God; about whom it is certainly agreed that, even though he had not been washed by the font of baptism, was cleansed by the spilling of his blood and was made worthy of entering the kingdom of heaven.

2. A SAINT'S EARLY LIFE (ST PATRICK)

His Confession, explained in a letter to the Irish. I, the sinner
Patrick, the most uncouth and least of all the faithful, and the most
contemptible in the eyes of many, had for my father Calpornus the
deacon, a son of Potitus, son of Odissus the priest, who lived in
the village of Bannavem Taberniae. For he had a country residence
nearby, where I was taken captive. I was then almost 16 years old. But
I was ignorant of God, and was led into Irish captivity, with so many
thousands of men, deservedly so, because we withdrew from God, and
we did not observe his precepts, and we were not obedient to our
priests, who were reminding us of our salvation. And the Lord brought
upon us the anger of his living spirit, and scattered us among many
peoples, even to the very ends of the earth, where now my humble
self seems to be among foreigners. And there the Lord laid bare the
consciousness of my disbelief, so that perhaps I might at last remember
my crimes and convert with my whole heart to my Lord, who took
account of my humbleness and pitied my youth and my ignorance,
and who looked after me before I knew him, and before I could
understand or distinguish between good and evil, and he protected
me, and counsels me, as a father does his son.

3. ST COLUMBA VS. THE LOCH NESS MONSTER (ADAMNAN)

Concerning the repulsion of an aquatic monster by the virtue of the
Saint's prayer. In another time, too, when the Saint was tarrying for
several days in the land of the Picts, he had need to cross the river
Ness: after he had approached its bank, he saw some of the locals
burying a wretched little man, whom, as the burial party themselves
recounted, a little while previously as he was swimming a certain
aquatic beast snatched and bit into him with a most savage bite;
whose miserable corpse, although too late, some of them coming to
his aid seized with long hooks. The Saint on the contrary, hearing
this, ordered one of his companions to swim out and sail back to him
a small boat which was standing on the other bank. Having heard
this order of the praiseworthy holy man, Lugneus Mocumin, obeying
without delay, and having taken off his clothes with the exception

of his undergarments, threw himself into the water. But the monster, which earlier had not been satiated as much as stirred up against its prey, was lurking in the depths of the river, perceiving that the water above had been disturbed by his swimming, the marine creature suddenly emerging rushed towards the man swimming in the middle of the channel with a huge roar and with gaping mouth. The Saint seeing this, while all who were there, both the heathens and even the brothers, were stricken by excessive fear, after he had drawn with his index finger, having raised his holy hand, the sign of the cross in the empty air, having invoked the name of God commanded the ferocious beast, saying, 'Approach no further, nor touch the man; quickly turn backwards.' Then indeed the beast, having heard the voice of the Saint, and as if he was being dragged by ropes, with a speedier retreat he fled back trembling; the beast which previously had approached right up to the swimming Lugneus, so that there was not between man and beast more than the length of one little pole. Then the brothers, seeing that the beast had retreated, and that Lugneus their comrade had returned to them safe and unharmed in the little boat, with great astonishment they glorified God in the Saint. And also the native heathens, who were there at hand, compelled by the magnitude of this same miracle, which they themselves had seen, praised the God of the Christians.

4. THE TRANSLATION OF ST CUTHBERT (SIMEON OF DURHAM)

There, having lifted up the covering which had concealed the casket, they did not dare to open it right away, but surrounding it with candles, carefully inspected it, if by chance through some cracks or any other indication they might have been able to detect what lay inside. But when nothing certain was revealed to those who were doing this, at length with the lid removed, although they were fearful, they saw a book of the Gospels placed at the head above the panel. And when they lifted the panel, and having removed the linen cloth which immediately behind the panel had concealed the sacred relics, they inhaled a fragrance of the sweetest odour. And behold! they discovered the venerable body of the blessed father, namely the fruit of their desire, which, lying on its right side, by its complete soundness and by the flexibility of its limbs presented to view more a sleeping than a dead person. Having seen that, they were overcome by a huge dread, and retreating a little further away, they did not dare to gaze upon the miracle which was revealed. On bended knees they began repeatedly to beat their breasts with their fists, and, with hands and eyes lifted on high, often to exclaim, 'Have mercy on us, O Lord, have mercy.' Meanwhile that which each had seen, and as if they had not seen it, each in turn announced to themselves. At length with their entire body prostrate, and tears copiously flowing, they humbly petitioned the Lord with the seven Penitential Psalms, not in his wrath to rebuke them, nor in his anger to chastise them. With these supplications completed, approaching on hands and knees rather by crawling than by walking on foot, they there and then caught sight of so many relics of Saints, that the narrowness of that casket could not have held them, except the sacred body of the father lying, as has been said, to one side, allowed them a greater space for resting together with him here and there. Undoubtedly it is agreed that those relics, as is read in ancient books, are the head of the glorious king and martyr Oswald, also the bones of the venerable confessors and priests of Christ, namely Aidan and the successors of the worshipful father Cuthbert, namely Eadbert, Eadfrid and Ethelwold. And in addition the bones of the Venerable Bede, who lucidly had written the life of Saint Cuthbert, had occupied this place of rest along with his body, which together a linen sack held. There were also found in the same place many relics of other Saints.

5. THE MARTYRDOM OF BECKET (EDWARD GRIM)

The unconquerable martyr discerning that the hour was at hand which would put an end to this mortal misery, and that the crown of immortality promised to him by The Lord was now coming near, with his neck inclined in the manner of one praying, and with his hands joined together and raised upwards, entrusted his cause to God and to the holy Mary and to the blessed martyr Dionysius and the church.

Hardly was this utterance completed, a wicked soldier, fearing that he would be snatched away by the people and escape alive, attacked him suddenly, and since the top of his crown, which the anointing of a holy unction had consecrated to God, had been shaved, he wounded the lamb being sacrificed to God on the head, and the arm of he who is relating this was maimed by the same blow. For he, while the monks as well as all the priests were fleeing, resolutely stayed close to the holy archbishop, and between his outstretched arms clasped him in an embrace, until that [arm] which was exposed was maimed. Then having received another blow on the head yet still he [Becket] remained motionless. But having been struck by a third blow the martyr bent his knees and elbows, offering himself as a living sacrifice, saying in a whisper, 'In the name of Jesus and for the protection of the church I am prepared to embrace death.' But the third soldier thus inflicted a serious wound on him while he was bending forward, with which blow both the sword struck against the stone and his crown, which was large, was thus separated from the head, so that pale blood from the brain (despite the brain being red from blood) stained the appearance of the church with the colours of the virgin and the mother, with the life and death of the confessor and martyr. The fourth soldier drove away those who were coming up so the rest could more freely and boldly perpetrate the homicide. But the fifth, not a soldier but a priest who had entered with the soldiers, so that the martyr, who had imitated Christ in the others, would not lack a fifth wound, having placed his foot on the holy priest and precious martyr's neck (horrendous to tell) scattering the brain with blood across the pavement exclaimed to the rest, 'Let us begone from this place, soldiers, that man will rise no longer.'

But amidst all this the famous martyr exhibiting the virtue of incredible constancy neither opposed his hand nor clothes, as is characteristic of human infirmity, to the assassin, nor having been struck down did he utter a word, nor emit a cry, nor a sound indicative of any pain; but he held his head which he had inclined to the roaming swords unmoving, until suffused with blood and brains, bending forwards as if for the purpose of praying, his body lay on the pavement, his soul in the bosom of Abraham.

Chapter 5

1. A MEDIEVAL VAMPIRE (WALTER MAP)

I am aware that a very notable prodigy occurred in Wales. William Laudun, an English knight, a man strong with courage and of proven boldness, came to Gilbert Foliot, then Bishop of Hereford, but now of London, saying, 'Lord, seeking advice I appeal to you: a certain wicked Welshman died quite without faith in my village recently, who straight away after four nights returning to the village on every successive night does not cease to summon singly and by name his fellow villagers. Those who are called are immediately weakened and die within three days, so that by now few remain.' The Bishop in wonderment said, 'Perhaps God has given power to an evil angel of the fall to rouse itself in that dead body. But let that corpse be exhumed, and having severed its neck with the spade let it and the grave be sprinkled with holy water, and let it be put back.' And although this was done nevertheless the remaining villagers were harassed by it with its former wandering. Therefore on a certain night, when by now it had left only a few survivors, it called William himself with a triple invocation. But he, as he was undaunted and indefatigable, nor unaware of what it was, leapt up with drawn sword, and having followed the fleeing demon right up to the grave, where already it was falling back into the grave he struck it on the head right up to the neck, and the persecution of the wandering plague ceased from that hour, nor thereafter did it harm William himself or any of the others. We know the true tenor of this matter, the cause we do not know.

2. A LUNATIC THEORY (ALEXANDER NECKAM)

Several people are investigating for what reason a certain shadowy stain may be seen on the moon. Hence some people are of the opinion that that the lunar body is hollow, in such a way that the moon's caverns cannot admit the rays of solar light into themselves. To others it seems that the body of the moon is not round, but that in certain of its regions is raised higher, in others lower. Therefore the regions which are low-lying in the manner of valleys do not feel the benefit of the solar light. But this conjecture is bordering on aforementioned conjecture. Others propose that the lunar body is dark in its own nature, in such a way that certain of its regions are naturally darker than others, whence they are not subject to illumination. But it must be known that this was done by way of a sign and an instruction for us. For deservedly by the transgressions of our first parents, the splendour of all the planets and stars sustained a loss of brightness. But the moon, which is in the vicinity of the earth, and most familiarly occurring to human sight, retains a stain on itself, for the purpose of indicating that for as long as we rush along in this state of our present life, there is some stain on the holy church. But when all the planets with the stars too will stand motionless as if having discharged their duties, our state will be stable, and there will be no stain on the lunar material, nor on the holy church likewise. Perhaps the naïve reader has taken no heed of what I call the moon's stain. Surely you know what the common man calls the rustic on the moon carrying the thorns? Whence one speaking vulgarly says:

> The rustic on the moon, whom one burden weighs down.
> Demonstrates by his thorns that stealing benefits no one.

Therefore as often as you see that shadow which has been scattered about, call to mind the transgression of our first parents, and groan. But presently through hope cheer yourself up, and heave a sigh for the glory of that state in which our bodies having been glorified will be brighter than the sun, which just as the rest of the planets along with the stars will be far brighter than it is now. How fortunate will be the conjunction of the body and the soul, which will be far brighter than the sun? O brightness unerring, o brightness desirable, o admirable beauty.

3. ON EXPERIMENTAL SCIENCE (ROGER BACON)

For there are two ways of knowing, namely through argument and experiment. Argument infers and makes us admit the conclusion, but it does not provide information nor remove doubt so that the mind rests in the consideration of truth, unless it discovers this by way of experience; so it is that many have arguments about what is knowable, but because they do not have experience they neglect them, and neither do they avoid harmful arguments nor follow good ones. For if some man who never saw fire proved by an adequate argument that fire burns and damages and destroys things, never could the mind of anyone hearing him rest because of this, nor would he avoid fire until he placed his hand or some combustible matter in the fire, to prove by experience what argument teaches. But the truth of combustion having been acquired by experience the mind rests in the brilliance of truth. Therefore argument is not sufficient, but experience is.

4. ON RAINBOWS (ROGER BACON)

For if two men stand looking at a rainbow in the north, and one withdraws westwards, the rainbow will move equidistantly to him, and if the other goes eastwards, the rainbow will move equidistantly to him, or if he stays still in his original place, the rainbow will stay still. It is evident therefore that a rainbow is counted according to the number of men looking at it; and so it is impossible that two men could see one and the same rainbow, although the unlearned do not perceive this. For the shadow of each [observer] divides the arc of the rainbow into two equal parts, and so, although the shadows are equidistant as far as can be perceived, they do not meet in the middle of the same rainbow, and so each individual rainbow is indebted to each onlooker. And this is evident, because if the two rainbows are moved into diverse and opposing places, they will be moved according to the motion of the observers, and so there are as many rainbows as there are observers. From these facts therefore it follows that the rainbow is not seen except through the reflected rays of the sun, because if it were through the incident rays then the rainbow would be a thing fixed in one place in the clouds, which would not vary according to the motion of the observer, nor according to the number of them.

Chapter 6

1. THE FIRST OF MAY (GEORGE BUCHANAN)

The Kalends of May. Hail the first of May, consecrated to sacred pleasures, to joy and wine, given over to games and jokes and to the delicate dances of the Graces. Hail, pleasure and the shining glory of the year returning in unending succession, and the flower of revived youth, rushing towards time's dotage. When the alluring mildness of spring first shone on the new world, and the new age glittering with yellow metal was inherently just without law, such an uninterrupted course throughout all the years soothed the lands with the warming west wind, and revived the fertile fields without seeds. Such a perpetual warmth of fortunate air lies over the blessed isles and the fields ignorant of troublesome old age and fretful sickness. Silently such a breath rustles with a whisper the silent grove of death and stirs the funereal cypresses beside forgetful Lethe waters. Perhaps when God will purify the world with final flames, and bring back happy ages to the world, such a breeze will soothe the heavenly souls. Hail, glory of the passing age, hail day worthy of favourable distinction, hail reflection of ancient life and sign of the coming era.

2. RICARDUS TERTIUS (THOMAS LEGGE)

MAID.

When will any time be devoid of disasters and will the grief of the stricken mother come to an end? For, insane, you cannot be silent about the sad news for the mother? Or does the mind rejoice to protract all its afflictions, and shut in long sorrows? O mighty queen, once swollen with royal pride.

QUEEN.

Unhappy woman, why are you struck dumb in the midst of speaking? Why cannot the sound which has been ordered out find a route? And your unsightly cheeks are sodden with pouring tears.

MAID.

The raging boar has savaged with its bloody tusk.

QUEEN.

Whatever crime still remains?

MAID.

Ah, your sons.

QUEEN.

I desire to hear my misfortunes immediately.

MAID.

Alas, both princes have been wickedly suffocated, her shaken mind succumbs: get up, woe is me, unhappy woman restore your falling spirit again. She breathes, she has revived, slow-moving death flees from the unhappy.

QUEEN.

Now you can reign, o wicked uncle, fierce fury will not fear unwarlike boys. May you brandish your wicked sceptre: still your crime lacks one thing, now seek my blood, I will not be the unhappy proof of your fury. Whom should I, wretch that I am, mourn? relatives? children? or he whom the fates allowed to survive such great evils? For I a mother killed my own sons, O Edward when I stripped your side of your companion, and then sweet boy you abandoned your refuge. I a supppliant mother on my knees unequal to the task pray that you, you who avenges, who hurls the flames, thundering father, let your darts be

hurled at this perjurer. May you in your anger lay bare Olympus with
your thunderbolts, and let the ruin of heaven punish the impious man.
MAID.

But let you think of peaceful things, soothe your soul, and heal your
disturbed mind, relieve your cares.

QUEEN.

O the uncle's abominable atrocity, such as frightful Procrustes did
not know, or the fearsome woman of Colchis. O deceitful faith of
an impious Cardinal, to whom madness entrusted my son. O dearest
sons, o children, whom the cruel sword of an uncle has snatched away,
nor does one unholy deed suffice for his wickedness. They refuse me
a mother your funeral.

3. IGNORAMUS (GEORGE RUGGLE)

IGNORAMUS: Fie, fie. Such a press, such a crowd that I'm almost
pressed to death; I will have an action of Intrusion against all of you.
Aha, Monsieurs, voulez vous intruder par ioyn-tennant? Fie, fie! I am
excessively heated, cha, cha! I pray God that I have not melted my fat; fie
fie! in the name of the Lord where are my clerks now? Dulman, Dulman.

DULMAN: Here Master Ignoramus, vous avez Dulman.

IGN: I am being melted, Dulman, melted. Rub me with a towel, rub.
Where is Pecus?

PECUS: Here, sir.

IGN: Make wind, Pecus, thusly, so, so; where is Fled-witt?

DUL: He is not to be found.

IGN: Now put your cloaks over me lest I catch cold. So, so, bien faicte.
Among all my injuries I am exceedingly glad and I rejoice now because
I have made a good agreement among our English; on that account
tomorrow we will hoist our sails and return once again to London; for
the time we came here was the Eighth of Hilary and now it is almost
the Fifteenth of Easter.

DUL: I swear, master, that you have tickled the point of the law today.

IGN: Ha ha, I think I will tickle it.

PECUS: Never have I heard a better tickling; what do you say, Musaeus?

MUSAEUS: Indeed, I understood little enough.

IGN: You are a *galli crista*, called 'a cocks-combe'; I will never make
you a lawyer.

DUL: Never, never, for he was a university man.

IGN: Those university men are great idiots and no kinds of clerics: I wonder how you spent your time among them.

MUS: For the most part I was engaged in Logic.

IGN: Logic? What village or town is Logic?

MUS: It is one of the liberal arts.

IGN: Liberal? So I thought, in the name of God study the thrifty and lucrative arts; this is no longer the world for liberal arts.

MUS: I was dedicated to the love of Philosophy.

IGN: To love? What? Are you in favour of baggages and strumpets? If you keep a bad rule, you are not for me, I will send you back again into the hands of your parents.

MUS: The gods will have done it.

IGN: What o'clock is it now?

DUL: It is between eight and nine.

IGN: Nine! Go therefore to our guest-house with the bags and scrolls, what is that? Let me see this instrument; wait un petit while I put my spectacles on my nose. Oho now I know: this is an indenture made between Roger Ratledocke of Caxton in the county of Brecknock. Oho, Richard Den, John Fen; oho, oho, Proud Buzzard plaintiff versus Pegoose defendant. Oho, here is a fault in the letter, correct it, correct it, for in our law one comma overturns the whole opinion. Go now, you copy this, you make a fair copy of this, you pack our belongings for the journey.

4. IN BARVITIUS' GARDEN (ELIZABETH JANE WESTON)

In the same person's gardens. Here highly cultivated with fragrant plants and nurtured by his constant effort is the garden of cultivated Barvitius. Here, whenever the court of Caesar releases you weary, you relieve your tired breast from the burden of your cares. Here too is a place assigned for faithful friends; here you are allowed to enjoy their sight and conversation. Here, in virtue of your inherent generosity, you are used to hearing the supplications of widows, and to take up the wishes of your clients. In this way the garden adorned with flowers serves its master: and the master rejoices in the grace of his own garden. What therefore might I ask for this? Let not the impetuous ferocity of the north or east winds drive away the gentle western breezes. But let it thrive so with a variety of fruits, and each year supply to its master acceptable gifts. And what might I ask for the master? Let not envy in the court harm he who is always accustomed to be the companion of virtue.

5. CRUEL FATE (GEORGE HERBERT)

While willingly I was prefering the short and pious path over the grand and guilty one, a malign star snatched away this modest aim and mixed wine with bitter bile. Thence every part of me cried out and severely I long to threaten the world itself; at last having companionably taken hold of my cloak someone whispers in my ear, this had once been the drink of your Lord. I taste the draught and approve it.

Chapter 7

1. ON THE BENEFITS OF MUSIC (JOHN CASE)

But to summarise the whole matter in a few words, the use of music is threefold: divine, which is concerned with contemplation, ethical, which is concerned with the system of life, political, which is concerned with the conservation of the state and of the citizenry. We have said enough about the theoretical and divine, now we will say a few things about the ethical and civil. The ethical or moral use of music (to proceed by making a distinction) is perceived in two things especially, to be sure in restraining evil emotions and in acquiring good morals: hence why Aristotle and other philosophers recommended that boys and adolescents ought to be compelled to study and practice music, of which matter there are three causes, because in it there is expressed the image and sweetness of virtue, the useful exercise of the voice, the moderation of emotion. The image of virtue: for music itself is a virtue; the virtue of sweetness, for music itself is harmony; the exercise of the voice, for in the practice of music there is a wholesome agitation of the lung, which begets a noble respiration and heat in the vitals, disperses the dense humours (in which the youthful age abounds), and drives out all vapours and mists flowing or which have flowed from the head; finally the moderation of emotion partakes in that, because as we have taught above, through the air and the ear it stirs the mind itself, and in an extraordinary way holds that under its own approbation and power.

2. AGAINST SUPERSTITION (FRANCIS BACON)

The human intellect, in support of those things which at one time were generally accepted (either because they have been received and believed, or because they are a source of delight), also draws all other things to support and be in agreement with them: and although there may be a greater force and abundance of instances, which occur on the contrary side, however it either takes no notice of them or despises them, or by drawing a distinction excludes and rejects them, not without a great and pernicious prejudice, so that their authority with its former erroneous conclusions remains inviolate. And so he rightly replied, who, when a picture hanging in a temple was shown to him of those who had fulfilled their vows, because they had escaped from the peril of shipwreck, and he was pressed by being asked whether then indeed he did not acknowledge the power of the Gods, he asked in turn, But where are those depicted who after their vows had been made died? It is the same method with almost all superstition, as in astrology, dreams, omens, divine retributions, and things of this sort in which men having taken delight in the vanities of such things take notice of the events where they are fulfilled; but when they fail, although much more frequently, however they neglect and pass them by.

3. ANTS, SPIDERS AND BEES (FRANCIS BACON)

Those who have had dealings with the sciences were either empiricists of dogmatists. The empiricists, in the manner of ants, only collect and use; the rationalists, in the manner of spiders, produce webs from out of themselves: but the bee is the middle ground, who gathers material from the flowers of the garden and field; but also with its own particular skill applies it and organizes it. And nor is the true work of philosophy dissimilar; because neither by the strength of the mind alone or entirely does it strive, nor does it place material produced from natural history and mechanical experiments in its memory intact, but in the intellect once it has been changed and tamed. And so out of a closer and purer federation of those faculties, namely experiment and reason (which has still not been done), we ought to have high hopes.

4. ON THE CIRCULATION OF THE BLOOD (WILLIAM HARVEY)

Concerning the amount of blood passing through the heart from the veins into the arteries and the circular motion of the blood. Thus far [I have spoken] about the transfusion of the blood from the veins into the arteries, and the routes through which it can pass and how from the pulse of the heart it is transmitted and distributed, concerning which matters perhaps there are some who, with their reasonings having been influenced previously by the authority of Galen or Columbus or of others, may say that they will give their assent to me; but now when I will have said those things that remain (although especially worthy of consideration) concerning the quantity and progress of that blood passing through, they are so novel and unheard of that I fear harm to myself not only from the jealousy of some but I am afraid lest I make all men my enemies, to such an extent does custom or learning once imbibed and fixed by deep roots, as if by second nature, prevail among all, and the slightest hint of antiquity compels veneration. At any rate, the die is now cast, my hope is in the love of truth and the candour of learned minds: indeed after I had often and honestly remarked to myself in a many-fold inquiry what great a quantity there had been, from the dissection, for the purpose of proof, of living animals, and the opening of arteries; both from the symmetry and magnitude of the ventricles of the heart and of the vessels entering and exiting (since no appearance is to no purpose, nature would not have allotted to these vessels in vain such a size in proportion) and from the arrangement and careful contrivance of the valves and lobes, and the rest of the fabric of the heart, and from many other things, and had for a long time turned over in my mind: namely what was the quantity of transmitted blood, in what short time was that transmission done, nor I had noticed was the fluid of ingested food able to supply its place, but that we would have empty veins, entirely drained, and arteries burst on the other side from the intrusion of too much blood, unless the blood in some way could make its way refreshed from the arteries into the veins and return to the right ventricle of the heart.

I began to consider with myself, whether it had a certain motion as if in a circle, afterwards I discovered that this was true and that the blood was thrust forward from the heart through the arteries into the material of the body and all its parts and was driven by a pulse from the left ventricle of the heart, in the same way as into the lungs through the arterial vein from the right [ventricles]; and again finds it way back through the veins into the vena cava and right up to the right auricle, in the same way as from the lungs through the aforesaid pulmonary vein to the left ventricle, as was said before. Which motion by that means may be called circular.

5. The three Laws of Motion (Isaac Newton)

Law 1: that every body perseveres in its own state of rest or movement uniformly in a straight line, except so far as it is compelled by applied force to change that state.

Projectiles persevere in their own motions, except so far as they are retarded by the resistance of the air and are impelled downwards by the force of gravity. A hoop, whose parts by a perpetual holding together draw themselves back from rectilinear motion, does not cease to be rotated except so far as it is retarded by the air. But the greater bodies of the planets and comets conserve for a longer time their own motions both progressive and circular made in spaces offering less resistance.

Law 2: that the change of motion is proportional to the motive force applied, and that it happens following the right line by which that force is applied.

If any force generates any sort of motion; a double force will generate double the motion, a triple force three times the motion, whether at the same time and once, or gradually and successively it will have been appplied. And this motion (because it is fixed always in the same region with the generating force) if the body was moving before, is either added to its combined motion or taken away from the opposing motion, or is mixed obliquely with the oblique motion, and is added together with that according to the directionality of each.

Law 3: that to an action there is always an opposite and equal reaction: or the actions of two bodies jointly together is always equal and is directed toward opposite parts.

Whatever presses or drags another, is just as much pressed or dragged by that. If someone presses a stone with their finger, their finger is also pressed by the stone. If a horse drags a stone bound with a rope, the horse is also dragged back (so to speak) equally toward the stone; for the rope stretched in both directions by that same attempt at slackening itself will urge the horse toward the stone and the stone toward the horse; and it will impede the progress of one as much as it advances the progress of the other. If some body impinging against another body, by its force in whatever way will have changed its motion, the same also in turn will undergo in its own motion the same change in the opposite part by the force of the other (on account of the equality of the mutual pressure). By these actions the changes become equal, not of velocities, but of motions; that is in bodies not otherwise impeded. For changes of velocities, made in the same way against opposite parts, because the motions are changed equally, are reciprocally proportional to the bodies.

Chapter 8

1. FABULA CANIS ET UMBRAE (JONATHAN SWIFT)

A puppy, while carrying food in his mouth gazes in the water, an image of a better morsel appears in the liquid: while he marvels for a long time at the unobtainable spectacle, and gapes open-mouthed high over the stream, the food from his mouth falls headlong to the depths of the swirling water, and at the same time its likeness snatches it away. Eagerly he catches at the shadow with deluded jaws; the image deceives him, and with his teeth he bites the air.

2. CANIS ET ECHO (VINCENT BOURNE)

With clear rays the silvery moon in the heavens shone reflected with quivering light in the waters of the Thames. Here a rascally puppy saw something malign, and snarling uttered shameless sounds in an unworthy manner: and having attacked the moon in the heavens and the moon in the waters, the savage dog rages equally against both planets. By chance beneath the further bank lay Echo, and the playful nymph heard the empty threats: she heard them; and the most charming champion decided to revenge fury with fury, and to return like for like. He, deceived by the copy of his echoing voice, is now more and more impatient of anger. Echo continues to return barks for barks; and what the dog started, the image only follows. At last when his jaws have become tired, and his spirit and voice too; his whole fury subsides, and the dog falls silent. Yet he could have been silent before; all foolish fury, and all futile anger returns upon itself.

3. To JOSEPH TAYLOR (ANTHONY ALSOP)

I have a cask born on the first of October, and enough of a leg of ham and flour; nor does my hearth or table or bed lack a suitable place. If you seek anything more than these, as luck would have it from time to time in the year I have a little bottle of wine, which a friendly ship, without the knowledge of the customs officer, brings. Wherefore come, enjoy these with me, and with the luxurious feast having been abandoned for a little while, become accustomed to a plain salt cellar and luxury bought for nothing. Here you will learn the many good things of a rustic life: here night is given to pure quiet, and the day passes without a lawsuit; in the morning no clients will disturb your sleep, or the cheerful entertainment of evening; here you will be able to live free from worries; and, but for the fact that your Phylis would be absent, happy in other things.

4. EPITAPH FOR A BELOVED CAT (JOHN JORTIN)

Wearied by years and serious illness, I, the gentlest Puss, am compelled at last to approach the infernal waters; and laughing Proserpina said to me, 'Henceforth you will have Elysian suns, Elysian groves.' 'But, if I have deserved well, indulgent Queen of the silent regions, allow me at least to return home for one night, to return home for one night, and to say to my master in his ear, "Even from beyond the Styx your Puss loves you faithfully".' Puss died in the year 1756. He lived 14 years, two months, four days.

5. RUNNING A FEVER (WALTER SAVAGE LANDOR)

While in a fever. If I am well, I would have agreed (I confess) to have abstained from medicines, and it irks me to leave my bedroom on a spring morning. A cure was at hand (alas no longer!) whose salvation she had offered to me: she closed the door never to return! But first she was not ashamed either to draw the sheets up to my neck nor to touch my forehead with the soft bloom of her hand, nor to wish to staunch with her cheek placed upon what she had inflicted, the vein gushing with precipitate blood: then (which she owes still) to promise rewards with this one stipulation, may I be patient, may I follow her orders well. O sickness! bringing fever and the sleeplessness of fever with you, O sickness come back, let her come back to he who is just now an invalid.

Chapter 9

1. ADVICE FOR A BEGINNER (FRANK LELIÈVRE)

The Muse, I reckon, tells her own followers to keep trying, even though she withholds sweet-sounding songs from our strings and, however much she is longed for, shuns our night-long labours. The flower of the growing rose is concealed in its own bud: hard flint hides the fire: and the Earth kept locked away in its inmost rock the brilliance of the emerald. But she rejoices, although tardily, to enrich the tenacious man: the spark of a struck flint is not hidden, nor is the flower of Love delayed for all time. You, carry on at any rate experimenting, for indeed you can, with harmonious words in your measures. The Muse will teach you while you are learning to amend your song with new understanding.

2. HAY FEVER (DAVID MONEY)

Summer fever, or mower's fever. Sneezing is a lucky omen (according to our ancient ancestors) able to signify that something good is at hand. Hence I am often blessed more than is my fair share: I enjoy many such portents and omens. For hay troubles my nostrils, together with the delightful flower, the harmless grass all over the fields harms my nose. Tiny particles strive by constant harrying to loosen mucus, so that all the phlegm rushes down in a rapid stream. I stifle the sound, until having drawn breath with raging nostrils I sneeze, or rather having seen the sun I sneeze at the same time. Will it end? I am uncertain, and I stand still with mouth gaping wide – I snee-, snee-,

snee-, snee-, sneeze again. Many sneezing attacks follow that sneezing attack (they spurn a delay) in a continuous series. What respite is there? I wipe my eyes, and I wipe my nose by washing, so that I have the sweet relief of cold water. Many things please me in the summer: but the mower's fever often drives away quiet love with a crash.

3. A THANK YOU (ARMAND D'ANJOUR)

> Untiring helpmate, five and twenty years
> you've scrutinised the Classics papers here;
> in checking texts in Latin and in Greek
> you've extirpated errors everywhere,
> producing every time in flawless form
> the final drafts: with this our thanks we bear.
> [Verse translation © Armand D'Anjour]

4. ON COOMBE HILL (MARK WALKER)

Walking on Coombe Hill: O delightful hill, to you I have awarded the prize of best place of all as I rove through your meadows: I wander everywhere with my little dog, while he capers here and there along rabbity paths, a happy companion. Now here arises the column, a proud monument overhanging the plain, in which the sonorous church rings clangingly. Summer shines cheerfully: playful breezes murmur through the trees or whisper among the bushes, or a wind increases suitable for flying breeze-blown kites: at the same time as our hearts fly up, worries tumble down into the patchwork fields.

5. JOYCE (FRANK LELIÈVRE)

Everything will partake of death: death snatched my Joy, but I do not complain: it does not come as a hardship for an invalid. It is a hardship nonetheless because it did not allow me to have rested beneath the eternal night united with my dear wife.

APPENDIX: MATTERS METRICAL

A brief summary of the rules of scansion and the various poetical metres encountered in this book. For more about Latin verse, see *Annus Mirabilis*, Chapters 2 and 3.

COMMON METRICAL FEET

In Latin quantitative verse, each line of a poem is said to consist of a specific combination of metrical 'feet' – the particular combination produces the particular verse form. Each 'foot' consists of heavy and light syllables, formed according to the rules given below.

iamb	˘ ¯	(light–heavy, 'di–dum')
trochee	¯ ˘	(heavy–light, 'dum–di')
spondee	¯ ¯	(heavy–heavy, 'dum–dum')
dactyl	¯ ˘ ˘	(heavy–light–light, 'dum–diddy')

SYLLABLE QUANTITY

• Syllables are either heavy (¯) or light (˘). Do not confuse with vowels, which are either long or short (see below)

• A light syllable contains a short vowel either on its own or followed by (a) a single consonant or (b) another vowel which does not produce a diphthong

• A heavy syllable contains (a) a long vowel (b) a diphthong (c) any vowel followed by two consonants, either in the same word or across two words. But if the second consonant of a pair is *r* or *l*, providing that the vowel in the preceding syllable is short, that syllable may be scanned as light

• A long vowel always produces a heavy syllable, but a heavy syllable can contain a short vowel (e.g. before two consonants)

• *h* does not count either as a vowel or consonant and is ignored for purposes of scansion

• *i* and *u* standing before a vowel in the same syllable are consonants (English *y* and *w*)

• *u* after *q* is not a separate vowel but part of a single (not double) consonant

• *x* and *z* count as double consonants (*x* = *ks*)

• If a word ending in a vowel or *m* is followed by a word beginning with a vowel or *h*, the final syllable of the first word is *elided*: that is it is 'knocked out' and not counted as part of the metre.